Your Complete HSP Superpower Guidebook:

Thriving as a Highly Sensitive Person

PUBLISHED BY: Lily Hart

Table of Contents

Introduction:
Embrace Your Sensitivity – Your Superpower Awaits!

Welcome to **Your Complete HSP Superpower Guidebook**. If you're holding this book, you're likely someone who has always felt a bit **different** in the world, someone who experiences emotions more deeply, notices the subtleties others overlook, and feels the weight of the world more acutely. You might have been told you're **too sensitive** or perhaps you've struggled to find your place in a world that often values toughness over tenderness.

But here's the truth: **Your sensitivity is not a weakness—it's your superpower.**

Being a Highly Sensitive Person (HSP) means you are wired to perceive and process the world in a way that others simply can't. Your heightened awareness gives you an edge in understanding the nuances of human emotion, beauty, and connection. You see the details that others miss and feel the beauty of life in ways that can be deeply enriching. **Your depth of empathy, creativity, and insight are extraordinary gifts** that can transform not only your life but the lives of those around you.

This book is here to help you recognize that what you may have once viewed as a burden is, in fact, the wellspring of your greatest potential. It's here to show you how to not just survive in a world that often feels overstimulating, but to thrive as an HSP.

Throughout these pages, you'll discover the science behind **sensory processing sensitivity (SPS)** and how it shapes the way you experience the world. You'll learn how to harness your unique traits to navigate relationships, make empowered decisions, cultivate creative pursuits, and build a life that honors your sensitivity rather than diminishing it.

You are not alone in this journey. Millions of people share your experiences, and with the right tools and mindset, you can unlock your true potential. **It's time to stop hiding your sensitivity or feeling that it's something to be fixed**. Instead, embrace it as your superpower.

Whether you're navigating the complexities of work, relationships, or personal growth, you'll find guidance here that helps you use your sensitivity to your advantage. By the end of this guidebook, you'll have a deeper understanding of your HSP nature and a clear path forward toward living a life that's aligned with who you truly are.

Together, we'll explore how to create a world that nurtures your sensitivities, how to build healthier relationships, how to make decisions that align with your heart, and how to turn your sensitivity into a source of strength and joy.

You are a deeply insightful, compassionate, and intuitive person. You have the ability to make the world a better place simply by being your true self. Your sensitivity is your gift.

Now, let's unlock your superpower and step into a life that celebrates and thrives on the beauty of your unique perspective.

Welcome to the journey. Welcome to **your** superpower.

Chapter 1:
The Science of Sensitivity

In a world that often celebrates loudness, speed, and assertiveness, it can be easy for those of us who are Highly Sensitive to feel out of place. We may have been told that we need to toughen up or that we are **"too emotional"** or **"too quiet."** But what if I told you that your sensitivity is not a flaw? What if it is, in fact, a gift—a superpower?

To truly embrace your sensitivity, it's important to understand what's going on beneath the surface. In this chapter, we'll explore the science behind what it means to be a Highly Sensitive Person (HSP). You'll learn about the biological and neurological factors that make you who you are, and how these traits, when understood and nurtured, can become your greatest strengths.

What is Sensory Processing Sensitivity (SPS)?

At the heart of being an HSP is something called **sensory processing sensitivity (SPS)**—a trait that affects about **15–20% of the population**. First identified by Dr. Elaine Aron in the 1990s, SPS is a genetic characteristic that means your nervous system is more sensitive to physical, emotional, and social stimuli. This sensitivity leads to heightened awareness and deep processing of the world around you.

SPS isn't a disorder; it's a temperament. Your brain and body are designed to pick up on subtle details, notice the emotions of others, and process information more deeply than the average person. In other words, you're more tuned in to the world, and you experience it on a richer, more complex level. While this can sometimes feel overwhelming, it's also what makes you insightful, empathetic, and highly attuned to the needs of others.

The Biology Behind Sensitivity

To better understand how sensitivity works, let's take a look at the science.

Researchers have discovered that HSPs have a **more active central nervous system (CNS)**, particularly in areas of the brain involved in processing sensory input and emotional stimuli. In simpler terms, your brain is naturally wired to notice and react to stimuli—whether that's a change in tone of voice, the faintest scent in the air, or a sudden shift in someone's mood.

One important study, led by Dr. Arthur Aron (Elaine Aron's husband and a psychologist), showed that when HSPs are exposed to stimuli (like images or sounds), there is more blood flow to the brain's **anterior cingulate cortex**, a region associated with processing emotions and making decisions. This heightened brain activity helps HSPs think deeply, reflect on experiences, and notice patterns that others might miss. However, it also means that HSPs are more likely to experience **sensory overload** or emotional overwhelm in environments that are too stimulating or chaotic.

So, if you've ever found yourself exhausted after a day of socializing, or overwhelmed by loud noises or bright lights, know that this is your nervous system doing what it's naturally wired to do: absorbing everything around you.

The Strengths of High Sensitivity

The trait of high sensitivity isn't just a random quirk—it's a valuable asset. Highly Sensitive People (HSPs) possess unique strengths that set them apart, particularly in the way they notice details and respond thoughtfully to their environment.

Studies show that HSPs are often more cautious and reflective, traits that help in avoiding unnecessary risks and making thoughtful contributions to any situation. With this awareness, HSPs can pick up on subtle shifts in their surroundings, whether it's a change in body language or a variation in tone, allowing them to understand others more intuitively.

Your sensitivity—your ability to notice subtle shifts in your environment—continues to be an asset. Your intuition and attention to detail help you navigate complex social dynamics, spot opportunities others might miss, and build meaningful, thoughtful connections. These qualities enhance your relationships, help you make informed decisions, and allow you to engage deeply with the world around you.

How Sensitivity Impacts Your Life

While the scientific background of being an HSP is fascinating, the real question is: How does this heightened sensitivity impact your everyday life?

1. Heightened Awareness:
One of the most significant aspects of being an HSP is your **deep awareness of the world around yo**u. This could mean noticing the subtle texture of a piece of fabric, the emotions running beneath the surface in a conversation, or the faint hum of a background sound that others overlook. This sensitivity allows you to gather more information and see things from a more nuanced perspective.

2. Emotional Depth:
Your heightened emotional sensitivity means that you can experience feelings more intensely. **You feel joy, love, and beauty more deeply**—but you can also feel sadness or stress more acutely. This can lead to deep, meaningful connections with others, but it can also make emotional experiences more challenging at times. Your empathy is one of your superpowers, allowing you to understand and comfort others in ways that are both profound and healing.

3. Overstimulation and Sensory Sensitivity:
On the flip side, this heightened sensitivity can also lead to **sensory overload**. Loud noises, bright lights, crowded places, or

too much stimulation can quickly drain your energy and leave you feeling overwhelmed. But this sensitivity also makes you more **attuned to your own needs**, which means you're able to take steps to recover and restore your energy when necessary.

4. Deep Processing and Reflection:

HSPs tend to be **deep thinkers** who analyze situations from multiple angles. This can be a strength when making important decisions or solving complex problems. It also means that you're more likely to have a rich inner world, filled with creativity, insight, and personal growth. However, this deep processing can sometimes lead to **overthinking** or dwelling on past events, so learning how to find balance and quiet your mind is key.

The Gift of Sensitivity

By now, you may be wondering: "What's the real value in all of this?" The answer lies in how **sensitivity enhances your life** in ways that others may not fully understand.

Your **deep processing** allows you to be a visionary—able to see possibilities others miss and understand the intricate details that make something beautiful or important. Your **empathy** enables you to connect with others on a level that can foster intimacy, trust, and mutual understanding. Your **creativity** thrives because you notice what others overlook and can weave disparate elements into something new and meaningful.

In fact, research shows that **HSPs are more likely to engage in creative activities**, such as writing, art, music, and problem-solving. This heightened creativity, paired with emotional depth and empathy, makes you an ideal collaborator, counselor, artist, or leader in fields where human connection and thoughtful innovation matter.

Being an HSP means that you **feel deeply**, think deeply, and care deeply. These are not qualities to hide or downplay; they are the foundation of who you are and the gifts you have to offer the world. When you embrace your sensitivity, you open the door to a life of connection, purpose, and fulfillment.

Conclusion: Embrace the Science, Embrace the Gift

Understanding the science behind your sensitivity helps you realize that you are not broken or flawed. You are wired differently—and that difference is a profound gift. The world needs people who notice, reflect, and deeply care.

By embracing your heightened sensitivity, you can begin to navigate your life in ways that honor who you are, rather than feeling overwhelmed by the challenges that come with it. As you continue through this book, remember: Your sensitivity is your superpower, and you are about to learn how to harness it to create the life you deserve.

Let's begin this journey of self-discovery and empowerment together. Your superpower awaits.

Chapter 2:
The Four Core Traits of an HSP

As we begin to explore what it truly means to be a Highly Sensitive Person (HSP), it's essential to understand the core traits that define this unique way of being in the world. These traits not only shape how you experience life but also hold the key to unlocking the full potential of your sensitivity.

Dr. Elaine Aron, one of the foremost researchers on the Highly Sensitive Person, has identified **four core traits** that are commonly present in HSPs. In this chapter, we'll dive into each of these traits and explore how they contribute to your strengths, challenges, and unique gifts. The goal here is to help you see how your sensitivity can be a powerful tool for thriving—not just surviving—in your day-to-day life.

Trait 1: Deep Processing

One of the most defining features of an HSP is the ability to **deeply process information**. While this might sound simple, it's actually a very powerful way of interacting with the world.

When something happens, whether it's a conversation, a new experience, or a piece of information, your mind doesn't just take it at face value. You **think about it deeply**—analyzing it, reflecting on it, and considering all its implications. You might find yourself mulling over a conversation hours after it's over or revisiting a piece of art again and again, discovering new layers each time. This deep processing can also make you highly introspective, as you often spend time reflecting on your own thoughts, emotions, and experiences.

This trait is tied to the way your brain works. Studies show that

HSPs have **more active brain regions** that process complex information, such as the **anterior cingulate cortex**, which is involved in thinking, decision-making, and emotional regulation. You're naturally inclined to **analyze situations in depth**, weighing all possible outcomes and considering different perspectives.

The Superpower of Deep Processing

While this can sometimes lead to **overthinking**, it's also what makes you an excellent problem solver, strategist, and decision-maker. Your ability to take in all the details and understand the bigger picture means that you can see solutions where others may miss them. Your deep processing also leads to **increased empathy**, as you can carefully consider how others might feel in a given situation. You think carefully before you act, making decisions that are thoughtful and aligned with your values.

How to Thrive with Deep Processing

- **Trust Your Thoughtfulness:** The depth with which you process information is a strength, not a flaw. Don't rush decisions; give yourself the time and space you need to reflect.
- **Find Healthy Outlets for Reflection:** Journaling, art, or quiet walks can help you work through your thoughts without getting lost in them.
- **Manage Overthinking:** While deep thinking can be a gift, it can also turn into overthinking. If you find yourself stuck in a mental loop, try grounding techniques like deep breathing, meditation, or writing down your thoughts to release them.

Trait 2: Emotional Reactivity

As an HSP, your **emotional reactivity** is heightened. When you feel something, you feel it deeply. Emotions don't just skim the surface for you—they **sink in**. This means that you experience both positive and negative emotions more intensely than others. A beautiful song, a tender moment with a friend, or an inspiring piece of art can leave you feeling elated and moved. Similarly, a difficult conversation, an injustice, or even a sad movie can have a profound emotional impact on you.

This intense emotional experience is also linked to the way your **nervous system** works. Research has found that HSPs have heightened levels of activity in the brain areas involved in **emotional processing**, like the **amygdala**, which is responsible for detecting threats, and the **insula**, which helps process feelings. For HSPs, emotions are a vital source of information, and your body naturally tunes in to them.

The Superpower of Emotional Reactivity

While emotional intensity can sometimes feel overwhelming, it's also one of your **greatest strengths**. Your emotional depth means that you're highly empathetic and can form meaningful connections with others. You're able to deeply understand people's feelings and offer them the kind of support and compassion they need. Your emotional awareness also makes you very **self-aware**, allowing you to tune in to your own emotional needs and act in alignment with your true self.

How to Thrive with Emotional Reactivity

- **Honor Your Emotions:** Allow yourself to fully experience your emotions, both the highs and the lows. **Give yourself permission to feel deeply**—your emotions are valuable signals that guide you toward understanding your true desires and values.
- **Practice Emotional Regulation:** Deep breathing, mindfulness, and self-compassion are great tools to help manage intense emotions. Remember, it's okay to feel what you feel, but finding ways to **center yourself** can help you navigate emotional challenges with grace.
- **Create Emotional Boundaries:** Being emotionally reactive means you're deeply affected by others. Protect your emotional energy by setting boundaries with people and situations that drain you.

Trait 3: Overstimulation

Overstimulation is one of the most common challenges that HSPs face. With heightened sensitivity, **too much stimulation—**

whether it's noise, bright lights, a crowded room, or even emotional intensity—can quickly overwhelm your nervous system. This overstimulation can leave you feeling **fatigued, anxious, or drained**.

The reason for this is simple: your nervous system is constantly processing more sensory input than others'. While this can make you highly aware of your surroundings, it can also cause your system to become overloaded if there's too much to process at once. This can happen in busy environments, chaotic situations, or even when you're experiencing multiple emotions at once.

The Superpower of Sensory Sensitivity

While overstimulation can be challenging, your ability to detect sensory details is a **gift**. HSPs are often highly **creative** and **intuitive** because of their sensitivity to the world. Your ability to notice the smallest details helps you create art, build relationships, and solve problems in ways that others can't. Additionally, your sensory awareness makes you **attuned to the needs of others**, allowing you to be a compassionate and insightful friend, partner, or coworker.

How to Thrive with Overstimulation

- **Know Your Limits**: Recognize when you're becoming overstimulated, and give yourself permission to step away from the situation. **Take breaks** and create spaces of calm to recharge.
- **Create a Calming Environment:** Surround yourself with soothing colors, sounds, and textures. This will help you regulate sensory input and maintain balance in your environment.
- **Practice Mindfulness and Grounding:** Techniques like deep breathing, walking in nature, or focusing on your senses can help you stay grounded and reduce the impact of overstimulation.

Trait 4: Empathy and Compassion

Perhaps one of the most heartwarming aspects of being an HSP is your deep **empathy**. HSPs are naturally able to sense and understand the emotions of others, often without them having to say a word. You can pick up on subtle body language, tone of voice, and energy in a room, giving you the ability to understand and connect with people on a deep emotional level.

This empathetic ability is linked to your **mirror neurons**—brain cells that fire when you observe another person's emotional state. Essentially, your brain **mirrors** the emotions of others, which helps you understand them on a visceral level.

The Superpower of Empathy

Your empathy makes you a **natural listener, caregiver, and friend**. People are drawn to your warmth and understanding because you have an innate ability to see their feelings and respond with compassion. Your deep empathy also enhances your relationships, as you are able to create emotional bonds that are authentic and meaningful.

How to Thrive with Empathy

- **Channel Your Empathy:** Use your empathy to build meaningful relationships, both in your personal life and in your career. Whether you're a counselor, a teacher, a friend, or a parent, your ability to empathize is a **unique strength** that allows you to help others in profound ways.
- **Protect Your Energy:** Empathy can be exhausting, especially when you absorb the emotions of others. Be sure to **set boundaries** to prevent emotional burnout, and give yourself time to recharge when needed.
- **Self-Compassion:** Show yourself the same compassion and understanding you offer others. It's important to care for your own emotional needs, too.

Conclusion: Embracing Your Core Traits

As you can see, each of the four core traits of an HSP—**deep processing, emotional reactivity, overstimulation, and empathy**—can feel challenging at times, but they are also profound strengths. When you understand how these traits shape your experiences and your gifts, you can begin to work with them, rather than against them.

In this chapter, we've explored how your sensitivity can guide you to a deeper understanding of yourself and others. It gives you the tools to process life in a meaningful way, form deep connections, and contribute to the world in ways that are uniquely yours.

As we continue through this guidebook, we'll explore how to embrace these traits and turn them into superpowers. But for now, remember this: Your sensitivity is not something to hide or suppress—it's something to celebrate, nurture, and cherish. You are exactly as you are meant to be.

Chapter 3:
Navigating Relationships as an HSP

Relationships are an integral part of the human experience, and for Highly Sensitive People (HSPs), they can be both one of the greatest sources of joy and, at times, of challenge. As an HSP, your ability to form deep, meaningful connections is one of your greatest strengths. But because you feel everything so intensely—whether it's the emotions of others, the energy in a room, or the nuances of communication—relationships can sometimes become overwhelming. The beauty of being an HSP lies in your ability to understand and connect on a level that many others cannot, but it also requires careful attention to ensure that you thrive in these connections without losing yourself.

In this chapter, we'll explore how to navigate relationships with family, friends, romantic partners, and even in professional settings, so that your sensitivity becomes a source of strength rather than overwhelm. We'll also discuss how to establish healthy boundaries, communicate effectively, and protect your emotional well-being while staying open to the intimacy and connection you crave.

The Unique Qualities of HSP Relationships

At the heart of every relationship is communication, and as an HSP, your style of communication is deeply attuned to emotions, subtle cues, and underlying feelings. This heightened awareness can make you an incredibly **compassionate listener**, someone who can offer emotional support in ways that make others feel truly heard and understood. You might notice shifts in someone's voice, body language, or mood long before they even realize it themselves, making you a reliable confidante and friend. You see the **full spectrum** of emotions, both in yourself and others, and this allows you to create bonds that are rich, meaningful, and deeply connected.

However, the very qualities that make you such a perceptive and empathetic partner can also make you vulnerable. Your **emotional reactivity**—a core trait of HSPs—can cause you to absorb the emotions of those around you, sometimes to the point where you lose track of where your feelings end and theirs begin. This can lead to **emotional burnout** if you don't take time to maintain your own emotional health. Understanding the dynamics of your sensitivity within relationships is key to fostering healthy, thriving connections.

Building and Maintaining Healthy Boundaries

One of the most important tools for thriving in relationships as an HSP is the ability to **set and maintain healthy boundaries**. Because you feel things so deeply, it's easy to get swept up in the emotions and needs of others. You might feel a strong impulse to help, fix, or support those you love, sometimes at the expense of your own well-being. But establishing clear emotional boundaries is essential for maintaining your energy and staying true to yourself.

What Are Boundaries?
Boundaries are simply the limits you set with others to protect your emotional and physical well-being. As an HSP, this could mean recognizing when you're feeling emotionally overwhelmed or overstimulated and giving yourself permission to step away from a situation, whether it's a social event or a difficult conversation. Boundaries also mean communicating openly and honestly with others about what you need, whether it's alone time, a calm environment, or emotional space.

The Superpower of Boundaries
When you set healthy boundaries, you're not only protecting your own emotional health, but you're also **teaching others how to treat you**. Boundaries help ensure that you can show up in relationships as your best, most authentic self. They allow you to

stay grounded and connected to your own feelings, so that you can be emotionally available to others without losing yourself in the process.

How to Thrive with Boundaries:
- **Know Your Limits:** Pay attention to your body and emotions. If you're feeling overwhelmed, exhausted, or drained, it may be time to step back and give yourself some space.
- **Communicate Clearly:** Express your needs to others with kindness and clarity. It's okay to say, "I need some quiet time to recharge," or "I can't handle this conversation right now, but we can talk later."
- Learn to Say No: Saying no isn't selfish—it's an act of self-care. You don't have to be everything to everyone. Prioritize what matters most and protect your energy.

Deepening Romantic Relationships

As an HSP, you are likely to crave deep, meaningful connections in your romantic relationships. You yearn for emotional intimacy, mutual understanding, and the ability to truly share your inner world with someone special. Your **empathy**, **emotional depth**, and **intuition** make you an incredibly caring and attentive partner. You're capable of sensing your partner's needs and feelings, sometimes even before they express them, which can create a profound bond.

However, relationships require balance, and for an HSP, navigating romantic relationships can present unique challenges. Because you feel emotions so intensely, conflicts can be difficult to handle. Small disagreements may feel overwhelming, and your heightened emotional sensitivity can make it hard to manage disagreements without feeling hurt or upset.

The Superpower of Emotional Depth in Romance
Your deep emotional capacity is a gift, especially when it comes to nurturing your partner's emotional needs. You're the kind of partner who values quality time, heart-to-heart conversations, and shared experiences. Your **ability to be present** and genuinely

attuned to your partner's emotions allows you to create a space of safety and trust in the relationship. You thrive in environments where emotional honesty is valued and where both partners are willing to listen and support each other's emotional growth.

How to Thrive in Romantic Relationships:
- **Communicate Openly and Honestly:** Share your feelings with your partner. Let them know when you need emotional support, alone time, or a deeper connection. Be honest about your emotional needs and sensitivities.
- **Handle Conflict with Compassion:** Disagreements are inevitable, but how you handle them makes all the difference. Approach conflict with understanding and empathy, and try to stay grounded in your own emotions, rather than getting lost in the heat of the moment.
- **Create Space for Emotional Recharge:** You may need time to process your emotions or unwind after a busy day. Communicate this need to your partner, and make sure you're both on the same page when it comes to finding time for self-care.

Navigating Friendships and Social Connections

Friendships are another vital area of life where your sensitivity can both shine and require care. As an HSP, you are likely to form **deep, soul-nourishing friendships** that are based on mutual respect, empathy, and emotional connection. You are the friend who will notice when something is off with someone and offer a listening ear, and your friends appreciate your authenticity and ability to really "**get**" them.

However, social interactions can sometimes be draining for you, especially in large groups or noisy environments. Because you're so attuned to the emotional states of those around you, you may find yourself absorbing their feelings, which can leave you feeling emotionally exhausted.

The Superpower of Connection
Your ability to form deep connections is one of the greatest gifts

you have to offer the world. Whether in small, intimate settings or close-knit groups, your emotional sensitivity allows you to bring out the best in others. You can offer **genuine empathy and insight**, providing a sense of safety and understanding that others cherish.

How to Thrive in Friendships:
- **Seek Like-Minded Friends:** Surround yourself with people who respect your sensitivity and who can offer the emotional depth and authenticity you crave in friendships.
- **Honor Your Need for Downtime:** It's okay to say no to social events when you're feeling overstimulated. Honor your need for solitude to recharge so you can be fully present with your friends when you are together.
- **Be Selective in Your Relationships:** Not all friendships will be healthy or fulfilling for you. Cultivate connections with people who understand and value your emotional depth.

Professional Relationships and the HSP

In the workplace, your heightened sensitivity can be both an asset and a challenge. Your ability to **notice subtle cues, work with detail**, and **show empathy** makes you an excellent collaborator and a supportive colleague. However, the fast-paced, high-stress nature of many workplaces can be draining for HSPs, leaving you feeling overstimulated, anxious, or even burned out.

The Superpower of Empathy and Attention to Detail
Your intuition and empathy give you a unique perspective in the workplace. You're often able to understand people's motivations and dynamics in ways that others miss. Your **careful attention to detail** and ability to work thoughtfully means you excel in roles that require precision, creativity, and deep focus.

How to Thrive in Professional Relationships:
- **Set Clear Boundaries at Work:** Recognize when your energy is being drained and take steps to protect it. If you need to take breaks or manage a more manageable workload, advocate for yourself.

- **Use Your Empathy to Lead:** If you're in a leadership role, your ability to understand and support your team will be one of your greatest assets. Cultivate an environment of open communication and emotional safety.

- **Find Work That Aligns with Your Sensitivity:** Look for professional roles or environments where you can use your empathy, creativity, and attention to detail without overwhelming yourself. Flexible, meaningful work will allow you to thrive.

Conclusion: Relationships as a Reflection of Your Sensitivity

As an HSP, relationships can be a double-edged sword—providing the depth, connection, and understanding you crave, but also requiring careful attention to protect your emotional well-being. By setting healthy boundaries, communicating openly, and honoring your emotional needs, you can create relationships that are enriching, supportive, and nurturing.

Chapter 4:
Embracing Emotional Intensity: Harnessing Your Inner Power

As a Highly Sensitive Person (HSP), one of the most defining aspects of your nature is your **emotional intensity**. Whether it's joy, sorrow, love, or frustration, you don't just feel emotions; you experience them deeply, profoundly, and with a kind of emotional depth that many others might never fully understand. While this capacity for intense emotional experience can sometimes feel overwhelming, it's also one of your greatest gifts. In this chapter, we will explore how to embrace and harness the power of your emotional intensity—turning what might feel like a burden into a superpower that enriches your life.

The Gift of Emotional Intensity

For an HSP, emotions are not mere reactions—they are a vibrant, intricate part of your experience. You feel things more acutely than most, and this allows you to engage with the world in ways that are richly nuanced and deeply meaningful. From the **ecstasy of a moment of connection** to the **heartache of a painful goodbye**, your emotions provide you with a complex, textured view of life. This emotional richness makes you an incredibly compassionate friend, partner, and confidant, as you are able to tune into the feelings of others with profound empathy.

But what happens when emotions become overwhelming? When the flood of feeling becomes too much to manage? For many HSPs, this is a real struggle. Your heightened emotional sensitivity can leave you vulnerable to emotional **overload** or **rollercoaster experiences**, where joy and sorrow seem to coexist in a delicate balance, sometimes making it difficult to know how to move forward without feeling consumed by your feelings.

The Superpower of Emotional Awareness
While emotional intensity can be difficult to manage at times, it also gives you **emotional awareness**—the ability to tune into your feelings in ways that can lead to self-understanding, growth, and connection with others. Your heightened emotional intelligence allows you to navigate complex emotional landscapes, both within yourself and in the relationships you cultivate with others.

This emotional awareness allows you to respond to situations with **empathy, insight, and compassion**, making you a valuable presence in the lives of those around you. Your ability to tap into deep emotions helps you understand the full scope of human experience, and this can be a powerful catalyst for creativity, healing, and problem-solving.

Understanding Emotional Overload

One of the challenges of emotional intensity for HSPs is the tendency toward **emotional overload**. When you experience emotions so deeply, you might find yourself becoming quickly overwhelmed, particularly in emotionally charged situations. This could manifest as feeling **drained** after a tense conversation, experiencing **anxiety** after a conflict, or even feeling deeply fatigued after prolonged social interactions.

Overload can occur when you are confronted with too much emotional stimulation at once—whether from other people's feelings, intense environments, or your own emotional turmoil. It's as though your nervous system is receiving more input than it can handle, and this can lead to a sense of emotional **exhaustion**, **frustration**, or **anxiety**.

The Superpower of Emotional Regulation
While emotional intensity can make you more vulnerable to burnout, the key to thriving as an HSP is learning to **regulate** your emotions. Emotional regulation does not mean suppressing

your feelings or pretending that everything is okay when it's not. Rather, it means **learning how to honor your emotions** and manage them in ways that support your well-being.

You have the capacity to **process emotions deeply**, and this ability to work through your feelings is essential for your growth and healing. But it's also important to recognize when it's time to step back, recharge, and restore your emotional balance before diving into the next wave of intense feelings.

The Power of Self-Awareness: Identifying Your Emotional Triggers

As an HSP, your emotions are often tied to deep-seated beliefs and past experiences, making it essential to become aware of your emotional triggers. These are the situations, people, or events that provoke particularly strong emotional reactions. For example, you might feel particularly sensitive to **criticism** or **conflict**, or you might have strong emotional reactions when others are upset. Understanding your triggers can give you a better sense of how to navigate emotional challenges with greater ease.

The Superpower of Emotional Intelligence

Your ability to identify and understand your emotional triggers is part of your **emotional intelligence**—the ability to not only recognize your own emotions but also understand why you feel the way you do. This self-awareness gives you the power to respond to situations thoughtfully rather than reacting impulsively. You can begin to recognize when your emotions are being triggered and take steps to **self-soothe** or **create distance** from overwhelming situations before they spiral into emotional overload.

By acknowledging your triggers, you can start to develop healthier coping strategies. Perhaps this means taking a break from a heated discussion, practicing deep breathing or mindfulness to calm your nervous system, or seeking support from a trusted friend or therapist to help you process challenging emotions.

Creating Emotional Resilience: Building Your Inner Strength

Building **emotional resilience** as an HSP is about learning to move through your intense emotions without letting them consume you. Emotional resilience doesn't mean you won't feel pain, sadness, or fear—it means that you have the tools to process and recover from these feelings, coming out the other side stronger and more grounded.

Emotional resilience is not an innate trait; it's something you can build and cultivate over time. Just like physical strength, emotional resilience comes from **practice** and **self-care**. The more you acknowledge and honor your emotions, the better you become at riding the waves of emotional intensity without being swept away by them.

The Superpower of Self-Compassion

Self-compassion is a key ingredient in emotional resilience. As an HSP, you may be prone to feeling **self-critical** or thinking you're "too much" for others when your emotions are intense. But it's important to remind yourself that your emotional depth is a **beautiful part of who you are**, not something to apologize for.

When emotions are overwhelming, practice self-compassion by speaking to yourself with kindness and understanding. Instead of berating yourself for feeling too much, try saying, "It's okay to feel this way. I'm doing the best I can, and I'm allowed to feel deeply."

Self-compassion helps you move through difficult emotions with grace and offers you the space to heal without judgment. By treating yourself with the same gentleness that you extend to others, you can create a safe, nurturing environment for your emotions to thrive.

Practical Strategies for Managing Emotional Intensity

Learning how to manage and channel your emotional intensity

will allow you to live more fully, without becoming overwhelmed by your feelings. Here are some practical strategies to help you harness the power of your emotional world:

1. Mindfulness
Mindfulness practices, such as deep breathing and grounding exercises, can help you stay present in the moment, reducing the risk of being swept away by your emotions. These practices help you observe your feelings without becoming attached to them, giving you the space to process them without reacting impulsively.

2. Create Emotional Timeouts
If you feel yourself becoming emotionally overwhelmed, give yourself permission to take an emotional timeout. Step away from the situation, go for a walk, or retreat to a quiet space where you can gather your thoughts and regain your composure. Use this time to **breathe deeply**, reconnect with your body, and allow yourself to calm down before returning to the situation.

3. Journaling Your Feelings
Writing down your thoughts and emotions can be a powerful way to process your feelings. Journaling gives you a safe space to express what's on your mind, helping you make sense of your emotions and gain clarity. Over time, journaling can also help you identify patterns in your emotional responses, giving you more insight into your triggers and how to manage them.

4. Engage in Creative Outlets
Whether it's painting, dancing, writing, or any other form of artistic expression, creativity offers you an outlet for your emotions. Creative activities allow you to channel your feelings in a productive way, transforming intense emotions into something tangible and meaningful. Plus, creativity can be incredibly therapeutic, helping you process emotions without needing to talk about them directly.

5. Seek Support When Needed
Sometimes, you may need help navigating your emotions. Seeking

the support of a trusted friend, therapist, or counselor can provide you with guidance, encouragement, and perspective. Talking about your emotions with someone who understands can lighten your emotional load and offer you new ways to cope.

Conclusion: Embracing Your Emotional Power

As an HSP, your emotional intensity is a reflection of your **depth, empathy, and compassion**. While it may feel overwhelming at times, your emotions are not a weakness—they are a powerful source of insight, creativity, and connection. By learning to embrace your emotions with compassion and mindfulness, you can turn emotional intensity into your greatest superpower.

Remember, you are not broken for feeling deeply. You are simply attuned to the vibrancy and richness of life. Your emotional world is a treasure, and by harnessing its power, you can live with authenticity, resilience, and profound connection to yourself and others.

Chapter 5:
Navigating the World of Sensory Overload: Protecting Your Energy

As a Highly Sensitive Person (HSP), one of the most defining aspects of your experience is your heightened sensitivity to sensory stimuli. The world around you—its sounds, sights, smells, and textures—can often feel more vivid, intense, and even overwhelming than it does for others. What might be a minor annoyance to someone else can feel like a sensory assault to you.

Whether it's the hum of fluorescent lights, the bustle of a crowded café, the overwhelming smells of a busy street, or even the emotional energy of people around you, sensory overload can quickly lead to feelings of exhaustion, anxiety, or frustration. While the world can sometimes seem too loud, too bright, or too chaotic, this chapter is designed to help you understand and manage sensory overload in a way that allows you to **thrive** without feeling drained. The goal is not to retreat from the world, but to protect your sensitive system so that you can enjoy life to the fullest, on your own terms.

Understanding Sensory Sensitivity and Overload

For HSPs, the brain processes sensory input—such as sounds, lights, and textures—differently than it does for non-HSPs. **Dr. Elaine Aron**, the pioneering psychologist behind the HSP concept, explains that highly sensitive people have a **deeper processing** of sensory information, which means they take in more details and experience stimuli more intensely. This can be a gift, as it allows you to appreciate the subtleties of beauty, art, and human connection. However, it can also mean that **everyday stimuli** can become too much.

Sensory overload occurs when your brain is flooded with too much information or stimulation, and your nervous system struggles to keep up. Common signs of sensory overload include:

- **Irritability** or feeling short-tempered
- **Fatigue** or feeling drained despite a full night's rest
- **Difficulty focusing** or concentrating
- **Feeling anxious** or "on edge"
- **Increased sensitivity** to noise, light, or touch

This sensory overwhelm can happen in public spaces like shopping malls, crowded social events, or even in the workplace. It can also occur in more intimate settings if the environment is too cluttered or emotionally charged. The key to managing this overload is recognizing that your sensitivity is not a flaw but a unique way of experiencing the world. And just like any superpower, it requires protection and careful handling.

The Superpower of Sensory Awareness

While sensory overload can feel overwhelming at times, your heightened sensory awareness is also a **superpower**. Your sensitivity allows you to notice details and nuances that others may overlook, such as the texture of a leaf, the subtle shift in a person's voice, or the mood of a room. This sensitivity can make you more attuned to the beauty and complexity of life. It is this awareness that allows you to experience the world in its full richness and depth, from the calming sound of a rainstorm to the vibrant colors of a sunset.

Your ability to detect and respond to sensory stimuli gives you **valuable insights** into the world around you. For example, you may be able to detect the emotional energy in a room, notice when something feels "off" in a conversation, or sense when someone is in need of support, all of which are powerful tools for building deep, meaningful connections with others.

However, in order to harness this superpower without becoming overwhelmed, it's essential to have **strategies in place** to protect your energy and manage the intensity of sensory input.

Strategies for Managing Sensory Overload

Here are several practical strategies to help you manage sensory overload and protect your energy:

1. Create Quiet Spaces
One of the most effective ways to manage sensory overload is to **create quiet, soothing spaces** in your life. These are environments where you can retreat to recharge and restore your energy when the world feels too overwhelming. This might be a corner of your home with calming décor, a favorite chair with a soft blanket, or a quiet outdoor space like a garden or park.

When you're feeling overloaded, retreating to a space that feels calm and comfortable can help your nervous system reset. This gives you time to **process sensory input** at your own pace and regain emotional balance before facing the world again.

2. Manage Your Environment
If you know you're heading into a situation that might trigger sensory overload (like a busy social event or a noisy café), take proactive steps to reduce the impact on your senses. Here are some ideas:
- **Use noise-canceling headphones** or earplugs in noisy environments.
- **Wear sunglasses or hats** to dim the intensity of bright lights.
- **Carry essential oils** or a small personal item, like a stress-relief ball, to help you ground yourself if things feel overwhelming.
- **Avoid crowded spaces** when possible, or take frequent breaks to step outside for some fresh air.

Your environment is one of the most immediate and controllable factors in managing sensory input. By adjusting it to your needs, you can prevent overstimulation and maintain a sense of calm.

3. Practice Grounding Techniques

When you start to feel overwhelmed, **grounding techniques** can help you return to the present moment and regain a sense of control. Some grounding techniques include:

- **Deep breathing**: Take slow, deep breaths in through your nose and out through your mouth. This helps calm your nervous system.
- **Body scans**: Focus on different parts of your body and consciously relax them, starting from your toes and working your way up to your head.
- **Mindful walking**: Walk slowly and pay attention to your surroundings—the feel of your feet on the ground, the air on your skin, the sounds around you.

These techniques help you reconnect with your body and the present moment, providing relief from the sensory overload that might be clouding your mind.

4. Limit Stimulation When Possible

While you may not be able to control everything in your environment, you can **limit stimulation** in ways that work for you. For example:

- **Set boundaries** around how much time you spend in stimulating environments, such as parties or shopping malls.
- **Minimize multitasking**: Doing too many things at once can overwhelm your senses. Instead, focus on one task at a time.
- **Take breaks**: Schedule short breaks throughout your day, especially during high-stress or sensory-demanding activities.

Limiting stimulation allows your nervous system time to recover and reduces the risk of reaching a tipping point where you feel overwhelmed.

5. Manage Social Energy

Social events and interactions can be particularly draining for HSPs, especially when there's a lot of background noise or emotional energy. Here are some tips to manage your social energy:

- **Give yourself permission to leave** when a social event becomes too much. You don't need to stay longer than feels comfortable for you.
- **Take solo breaks** during social events. Step outside, find a quiet spot, or just take a few moments to yourself to recalibrate.
- **Schedule downtime after social engagements**. Make sure you have time to recover from social events by scheduling a quiet evening or time to relax.

By being mindful of your social energy and planning accordingly, you can engage meaningfully with others without draining yourself.

Self-Care Practices for Sensory Protection

Self-care is vital for HSPs in managing sensory overload and maintaining your emotional and physical well-being. Here are some self-care practices that can help protect your energy:

1. **Sensory Self-Care**: Engage in activities that soothe your senses, such as taking a warm bath with calming scents, listening to soft music, or practicing yoga. These activities can help reset your sensory system and provide a sense of comfort and relaxation.

2. **Sleep Hygiene**: Good sleep is essential for recharging your energy. Ensure your bedroom is a peaceful, quiet space with minimal distractions. Try to establish a calming bedtime routine, such as reading, meditating, or listening to calming music before sleep.

3. **Nourishing Your Body**: A healthy diet and regular physical activity are important for maintaining balance and resilience. Eating nourishing, whole foods and engaging in gentle movement like walking, stretching, or yoga can help stabilize your energy and prevent sensory overwhelm.

4. **Mindfulness**: Regular meditation practice helps build emotional resilience and teaches you to observe your sensory

experiences without becoming overwhelmed by them. It cultivates awareness, helping you detach from external stimuli and ground yourself in the present moment.

5. **Time in Nature**: Nature has a calming effect on the nervous system. Spending time outdoors, whether it's a walk in the park, hiking in the woods, or sitting by the beach, can help you recharge and reset your sensory balance.

Conclusion: Protecting Your Sensory Superpower

Your sensitivity to sensory stimuli is not a limitation; it is a **superpower** that allows you to experience life in profound and beautiful ways. By understanding the dynamics of sensory overload and implementing strategies to protect your energy, you can continue to embrace your sensitivity and live a rich, fulfilling life.

Remember, you don't have to navigate the world on your own terms; you have the ability to adapt your environment and create spaces that allow your sensitive nature to thrive. By honoring your sensory needs, setting boundaries, and practicing self-care, you'll find that the world is a much more manageable and enjoyable place to navigate. Your sensitivity is a strength—embrace it, protect it, and let it guide you to a life full of connection, creativity, and balance.

Chapter 6:
The Power of Deep Connections: Navigating Adult Relationships as an HSP

As a Highly Sensitive Person (HSP), one of your greatest gifts is your capacity for **deep, meaningful connections** with others. Your heightened sensitivity allows you to perceive emotions and nuances in relationships that many people miss. You can sense the unspoken, feel the emotional currents beneath the surface, and empathize with the feelings of those around you. This ability makes you an extraordinary friend, partner, and confidant.

However, it's not always easy to navigate relationships when you feel emotions so intensely. Whether it's the vulnerability of intimacy, the complexities of communication, or the challenge of balancing your needs with the needs of others, being in relationships can sometimes feel like walking a tightrope.

In this chapter, we'll explore how to **navigate adult relationships as an HSP** in a way that honors your sensitivity while allowing you to thrive. We will focus on the strengths you bring to relationships and provide strategies for fostering deep, loving connections without compromising your emotional well-being.

The Superpower of Emotional Empathy

As an HSP, one of your most profound strengths in relationships is your **emotional empathy**. You are not just emotionally aware of your own feelings; you are deeply attuned to the emotions of others. Whether it's the subtle shift in tone during a conversation, the pain behind a partner's eyes, or the discomfort in a friend's posture, you can read emotional cues with remarkable accuracy.

This deep empathy enables you to form **genuine, close connections** with others. You can offer comfort, understanding, and support in ways that are truly meaningful. Your ability to listen with presence and validate others' feelings makes you a sought-after friend and partner.

However, it's essential to recognize that your empathy is a gift that requires careful management. When you are constantly attuned to the emotions of others, you might find yourself absorbing their feelings, sometimes at the expense of your own emotional well-being. This is where boundaries become crucial.

The Role of Boundaries in Healthy Relationships

Setting **healthy emotional boundaries** is one of the most important tools an HSP can use to preserve their energy and protect their emotional space. While your empathetic nature allows you to connect deeply with others, it also means you are more susceptible to taking on their emotional burdens.

Boundaries aren't about distancing yourself from others; they're about protecting your emotional reserves so you can show up as your best self in relationships. Here are some key points to help you set and maintain healthy boundaries:

- **Know your limits**: Understand what situations or people drain you the most. Is it being around negative energy? Is it taking on someone else's stress or pain? Recognizing when you feel emotionally overloaded is the first step toward protecting yourself.
- **Communicate openly**: Don't be afraid to communicate your emotional needs with the people you care about. If you need space or time to recharge, let them know. If a certain situation is

too overwhelming, it's okay to say so.

- **Create time for self-care**: Make time for yourself regularly, especially after emotionally intense interactions. Whether it's reading a book, taking a walk, or simply being alone for a bit, these moments allow you to recharge and recalibrate your emotional energy.

Remember, boundaries are about taking care of yourself so that you can give more fully to others without losing yourself in the process.

Managing Conflict and Sensitivity in Relationships

For many HSPs, conflict in relationships can feel particularly challenging. Because you feel emotions so deeply, arguments or disagreements can be emotionally overwhelming, and you may tend to **internalize** them more than others. At times, you may even feel like a conflict is a reflection of your worth or a sign that the relationship is in jeopardy.

However, **conflict** is an inevitable part of any relationship. It doesn't have to be something you fear or avoid. In fact, when handled with care, conflict can actually **strengthen** relationships. The key is learning how to manage conflict in a way that respects your sensitive nature while fostering deeper understanding and intimacy.

Here are some strategies for handling conflict effectively as an HSP:

1. **Pause before reacting**: Because HSPs tend to feel emotions deeply, your first reaction might be to become upset or withdraw. If you feel yourself becoming overwhelmed during a disagreement, it's okay to take a brief break to collect your thoughts and calm down before continuing the conversation.

2. **Communicate your feelings**: Use **I-statements** to express your emotions without blaming the other person. For example, "I feel overwhelmed when we argue in public," or "I need some

quiet time to process before we talk more about this." This approach allows you to communicate your needs without escalating the conflict.

3. **Practice active listening**: HSPs often excel at listening, but it's important to listen to understand, not just to empathize. Give your partner or friend the space to share their perspective fully before responding. This helps prevent misunderstandings and promotes mutual respect.

4. **Let go of perfectionism**: If you find yourself overanalyzing every detail of an argument or trying to fix things immediately, practice **self-compassion**. Relationships aren't about being perfect—they're about growing together. It's okay to make mistakes and have disagreements. What matters is how you learn and grow from them.

5. **Recognize when to seek outside help**: If you and your partner or friend are stuck in a cycle of conflict that feels unresolvable, it may be helpful to seek guidance from a therapist or counselor. Sometimes, having a neutral third party can provide a fresh perspective and help you navigate challenges with greater ease.

The Superpower of Sensitivity in Romantic Relationships

When it comes to romantic relationships, your **emotional sensitivity** can be both a gift and a challenge. Your capacity to connect deeply with a partner can foster an incredibly rich and intimate relationship, but it can also make you more vulnerable to emotional pain or disappointment. As an HSP, you may feel emotions in your romantic life with greater intensity, and this can sometimes lead to heightened fears of rejection or feelings of insecurity.

However, your sensitivity also makes you **highly attuned** to the emotional needs of your partner. You can be incredibly **nurturing**, attentive, and caring, making you a loving and supportive partner. Here are some ways to use your sensitivity as a superpower in romantic relationships:

1. **Be open about your needs**: In order for a romantic relationship to thrive, both partners need to understand and respect each other's emotional needs. Don't be afraid to communicate your desire for emotional intimacy, connection, and downtime. This transparency helps your partner understand you better and can prevent misunderstandings.

2. **Nurture emotional intimacy**: Your sensitivity allows you to cultivate a deep emotional connection with your partner. Take time to nurture this connection through meaningful conversations, shared experiences, and mutual vulnerability. These moments strengthen the bond and make the relationship feel more fulfilling.

3. **Practice self-soothing techniques**: In romantic relationships, disagreements or hurt feelings are inevitable. Practice self-soothing techniques such as mindfulness or deep breathing when emotions run high. This allows you to stay grounded and prevents you from being swept away by negative emotions.

4. **Respect your partner's emotional space**: Just as you need emotional space to recharge, your partner might too. Be mindful of their needs for alone time, and don't take it personally. Healthy relationships are built on mutual respect for each other's emotional boundaries.

5. **Embrace your uniqueness**: Remember, your sensitive nature is not something to apologize for. In fact, it is a beautiful quality that makes you a loving, compassionate partner. Embrace it, and let your unique emotional depth be the foundation of a strong, resilient relationship.

The Superpower of Deep Friendships

In addition to romantic relationships, your capacity for deep empathy and connection shines through in your friendships. As an HSP, you're the friend who listens without judgment, who offers comfort when times are tough, and who celebrates others' successes with genuine joy. Your friendships are likely filled with **authenticity** and **mutual care**, and you have a gift for creating spaces where others feel safe to be themselves.

However, because of your depth of feeling, friendships can also be a source of emotional strain if not nurtured carefully. **Emotional burnout** can happen if you give too much of yourself without taking the time to recharge, and you may also find yourself overwhelmed by friends who are going through challenging times.

Here are some ways to protect your emotional energy while nurturing your friendships:

1. **Set expectations**: Communicate with your friends about your needs. Let them know when you need emotional space, or if you're feeling overwhelmed by their personal struggles. True friends will understand and appreciate your honesty.

2. **Practice reciprocal care**: Friendships are built on mutual support. While you are naturally empathetic and caring, make sure that the energy flows both ways. Make sure your needs are also being met, and that you have the opportunity to be cared for in return.

3. **Engage in self-care**: Regular self-care is crucial for maintaining healthy friendships. Take time for yourself between social gatherings, and make sure you're practicing activities that help you recharge, such as journaling, taking walks, or meditating.

Conclusion: Thriving in Relationships as an HSP

As an HSP, your ability to connect deeply with others is a profound gift. The depth of your emotions, your empathy, and your intuition allow you to form relationships that are rich, authentic, and meaningful. By understanding your sensitivity and setting boundaries that protect your emotional well-being, you can build and maintain relationships that are not only fulfilling but also sustainable.

Remember that your sensitivity is not a weakness—it is a superpower that enables you to form profound bonds, offer healing to those around you, and create a life filled with meaningful connections. By nurturing your relationships and caring for yourself in the process, you'll continue to thrive, surrounded by love, empathy, and mutual respect.

Chapter 7:
Sensitivity and Decision-Making: Trusting Your Inner Compass

As a Highly Sensitive Person (HSP), you likely approach decision-making differently than others. While some people may make decisions quickly and decisively, you tend to feel the weight of your choices more acutely. You consider the emotional, ethical, and practical implications of your actions, often with a deep sense of responsibility toward others and yourself. This capacity for reflection and thorough consideration is part of what makes you such a thoughtful and conscientious person.

However, this same depth of feeling can also lead to **overthinking** or **second-guessing** yourself, especially when the stakes are high. You might find it challenging to make decisions quickly, and the pressure to get it "right" can leave you feeling anxious or paralyzed. At times, your sensitivity may make you overly concerned with the potential consequences of your choices, leading to self-doubt.

In this chapter, we will explore how to harness your sensitivity in decision-making as a **superpower**, so you can trust your inner compass, make choices with confidence, and avoid becoming overwhelmed by the process. Your sensitivity, when managed properly, can help you navigate life's decisions with **clarity**, **integrity**, and a deep sense of purpose.

The Superpower of Deep Reflection

One of the core strengths of being an HSP is your ability to **reflect deeply** on your experiences, emotions, and the possible outcomes of your decisions. This allows you to take a holistic approach to problem-solving, considering not only the facts but also the emotional impact on yourself and others.

Your ability to reflect deeply means you have an exceptional understanding of the **long-term effects** of your choices. While others might focus on immediate benefits, you naturally weigh the emotional, social, and ethical ramifications of your actions. This depth of thought is a powerful asset because it helps you make decisions that are aligned with your **values** and your long-term vision.

However, this deep reflection can also lead to **analysis paralysis**. The more you think, the more possible outcomes you can imagine, which can make it hard to come to a conclusion. The key here is to recognize that your reflective nature doesn't have to trap you in endless cycles of contemplation. You can use it to guide you toward decisions that are thoughtful, intentional, and true to who you are.

Recognizing the Signs of Overthinking

Overthinking can be one of the challenges that comes with being an HSP, particularly when you're faced with important decisions. While it's natural for you to want to explore all possible outcomes and make the most informed decision, sometimes this tendency can spiral into self-doubt and overwhelm.

Signs that you might be overthinking include:

- **Constantly second-guessing yourself**: Even after you've made a decision, you may find yourself revisiting the same thoughts and wondering if you made the right choice.
- **Procrastination**: The fear of making the wrong decision might paralyze you, leading you to avoid making any decision at all.
- **Physical symptoms of anxiety**: Overthinking can take a physical toll, leading to tension, headaches, or digestive issues.
- **Feeling emotionally drained**: The weight of constantly analyzing every possibility can leave you feeling exhausted or overwhelmed, making it difficult to move forward.

To overcome overthinking, it's important to recognize when you're stuck in a cycle of self-doubt and to employ strategies that allow you to ground yourself in the present moment.

Strategies for Confident Decision-Making

Even though your sensitivity might make decision-making feel daunting at times, there are several strategies you can use to feel more confident and empowered in the process. These techniques will help you connect with your **inner wisdom** and trust yourself as you make decisions.

1. Tune into Your Intuition

As an HSP, you have a natural gift for **intuition**. Your heightened sensitivity allows you to pick up on subtle cues that others might miss—whether it's a gut feeling about a situation or a sense of knowing about the best course of action. Trusting your intuition can help guide you through difficult decisions with a sense of clarity.

When you're faced with a decision, take a moment to quiet your mind and listen to your body. Does a particular choice feel "right" to you, even if you can't explain why? Do you feel a sense of discomfort or unease with another option? Your body often holds the answers that your mind may be overcomplicating.

Intuition doesn't always provide a detailed roadmap, but it can offer a sense of **peace** or **discomfort** that can guide your choices. The more you learn to trust your intuitive sense, the more confident you will feel in your decision-making process.

2. Break Down Big Decisions into Smaller Steps

Sometimes the sheer magnitude of a decision can be overwhelming, especially for HSPs who tend to weigh every possible outcome. To reduce this overwhelm, try **breaking down larger decisions** into smaller, more manageable steps.

For example, if you're making a career decision, instead of thinking about all the potential consequences of each option, focus on one step at a time:
- Researching job opportunities
- Talking to people in the field
- Listing your values and priorities
- Considering how each choice aligns with your long-term goals

By taking small, deliberate steps, you can avoid becoming overwhelmed by the enormity of the decision and gain clarity as you move forward.

3. Set a Time Limit for Decision-Making

One way to avoid overthinking is to set a **time limit** for making decisions. Instead of allowing yourself endless time to deliberate, give yourself a specific window of time to make the decision—whether it's an hour, a day, or a week. During this time, allow yourself to reflect and gather the information you need, but commit to making a decision by the end of the set time period.

This approach can help you **balance reflection** with action, encouraging you to trust the information and insights you've gathered without getting stuck in analysis paralysis.

4. Use Your Support System Wisely

As an HSP, you may feel the need to seek external validation or advice from others, especially when making big decisions. While it's helpful to get input from trusted friends, family, or mentors, it's also important to avoid **over-relying** on others' opinions. Too many conflicting viewpoints can overwhelm you and cloud your own judgment.

Instead, **use your support system strategically**:
- Seek advice from those who genuinely understand your values and sensitivities.
- Listen to others' perspectives, but always bring the focus back

to what feels **authentically aligned** with you.
- Create a safe space for yourself to process your feelings without feeling pressured to make a decision quickly.

Your support system can provide helpful insight and validation, but ultimately, you are the best person to make decisions about your own life.

5. Practice Self-Compassion

Finally, one of the most important strategies for confident decision-making is practicing **self-compassion**. As an HSP, you may have high expectations for yourself and feel a great deal of responsibility for making the "right" choice. However, perfection is not required—and sometimes the "right" choice is the one that feels best for you in the moment, even if it isn't perfect.

If you make a decision that doesn't work out as expected, allow yourself to learn and grow from it without judgment. Treat yourself with the same kindness and understanding that you would offer a close friend who was in a similar situation. Self-compassion helps you navigate life's decisions with a sense of calm and resilience, knowing that you can adjust and adapt as needed.

The Superpower of Aligning Decisions with Your Values

At the core of your decision-making process is a deep connection to your **values**. Because HSPs tend to be more introspective, you often have a clear understanding of what truly matters to you— whether it's family, integrity, creativity, or personal growth. Your sensitivity to the world around you gives you a strong moral compass, allowing you to make decisions that are aligned with your **authentic self**.

When you approach decision-making through the lens of your values, you give yourself a powerful tool for clarity. You don't need to have all the answers upfront; instead, focus on the core principles that guide your choices. Whether you're deciding on a

job, a relationship, or a personal project, ask yourself:
- Does this align with my values?
- How does this decision make me feel about myself?
- Does this bring me closer to the life I want to create?

By trusting your values as your guiding light, you empower yourself to make decisions with confidence, knowing that your choices are authentic and true to your heart.

Conclusion: Embracing Your Sensitivity as a Guide

Decision-making may never be a simple, fast process for you, but that doesn't mean it's a flaw. In fact, your ability to deeply reflect, carefully consider, and feel the emotional weight of your choices is what allows you to make decisions that are rich with purpose and authenticity. By embracing your sensitivity and trusting your inner compass, you can navigate life's decisions with confidence and clarity.

Remember, you are not alone in feeling the weight of your choices—you are a thoughtful, conscientious person with a remarkable ability to make decisions that reflect your deepest values. Trust yourself, practice patience, and allow your sensitivity to guide you toward the life that feels true to you.

Chapter 8:
The Gift of Emotional Awareness: Managing Intimacy and Sexuality as an HSP

As a Highly Sensitive Person (HSP), your ability to feel emotions deeply is one of your most remarkable traits. You experience the full spectrum of feelings—joy, sadness, excitement, and love—with an intensity that is both a gift and a challenge, especially when it comes to intimacy and sexuality. You're attuned to the emotional undertones of every relationship, and this includes your romantic and sexual connections. For you, intimacy is not just physical; it's emotional, spiritual, and deeply personal.

While this emotional awareness can lead to incredibly fulfilling and authentic relationships, it can also be overwhelming at times. The vulnerability required in intimate connections may sometimes trigger feelings of insecurity, fear, or anxiety. The key is learning how to embrace and channel your sensitivity in ways that allow you to experience intimacy and sexuality as **empowered, fulfilling** parts of your life.

In this chapter, we will explore how to understand and manage the emotional dimensions of intimacy and sexuality as an HSP. By honoring your unique sensitivities and creating the conditions for a nurturing and positive sexual and emotional life, you can transform these aspects into powerful sources of joy and connection.

The Superpower of Emotional Connection in Intimacy

For you as an HSP, intimacy is not a shallow or casual experience—it's an opportunity to form a deep and **meaningful emotional connection**. You crave authentic, soul-deep interactions where you feel understood, valued, and seen. The emotional bond you share with a partner enhances the physical experience, making sex not just an act of pleasure, but also an expression of love, trust, and emotional closeness.

This depth of emotional connection is a beautiful gift. It allows you to experience intimacy with a richness that many people might not understand or appreciate. For you, a simple touch, a soft word, or a shared moment of vulnerability carries immense meaning. You can feel your partner's emotions and moods, sometimes even before they do, which makes you an incredibly attuned and compassionate lover.

However, this heightened emotional sensitivity can also make intimacy feel more vulnerable. You may feel deeply impacted by the emotional energy of your partner, and if that energy is negative or conflicted, it can leave you feeling drained or unsettled. This makes it all the more important to prioritize emotional **safety** and **trust** in your intimate relationships.

Navigating Vulnerability and Emotional Safety

The emotional vulnerability required in intimate relationships can be both exhilarating and frightening for an HSP. The thought of opening up to someone, whether emotionally or physically, can stir up fear of rejection or being hurt. These fears are natural—after all, intimacy means allowing someone to see the most intimate parts of yourself. Yet, it's important to recognize that your sensitivity can be a source of **strength** in relationships, rather than a liability.

To cultivate emotional safety in intimacy, here are a few strategies that can help:

1. Choose Partners Who Honor Your Sensitivity

Because you experience emotions so intensely, it's crucial to be in relationships with people who **respect** and **understand** your sensitivities. In a romantic or sexual relationship, this means choosing a partner who is emotionally available, open to communication, and empathetic to your needs.

It's okay to take your time in getting to know someone before you open up fully. Trust is built over time, and it's important to feel safe and secure with a partner before diving into the deeper aspects of intimacy. Having a partner who respects your pace and boundaries will help you navigate the vulnerability of intimacy with confidence.

2. Set Clear Emotional and Physical Boundaries

Boundaries are essential in any relationship, but for an HSP, they are particularly important in **intimate** and **sexual** situations. Because you experience emotions so profoundly, you may feel overwhelmed or drained if your boundaries aren't respected. It's important to be clear with yourself and your partner about your emotional and physical needs.

Take time to reflect on what makes you feel safe and comfortable in intimate situations. Are there certain physical touch points that feel especially comforting or overwhelming? Do you need emotional reassurance or verbal communication during intimate moments? The more you communicate these needs, the more likely it is that your partner will meet them, allowing you to enjoy intimacy without feeling anxious or misunderstood.

Also, remember that boundaries aren't just for protecting your emotions—they also help you maintain a sense of **personal integrity**. Setting boundaries allows you to engage in intimate situations that feel empowering, not draining. Boundaries create the emotional container that allows you to give and receive love freely, without fear of losing yourself in the process.

3. Be Patient with Your Emotional Process

As an HSP, you may find that intimacy triggers an emotional process for you that takes time to fully integrate. After a deep emotional connection or sexual experience, you might need time to reflect, process, and come to terms with your feelings. This can be especially true if you've felt overwhelmed or if the experience has stirred up deep emotions.

Allow yourself the space to **process** your emotions without judgment. It's perfectly okay to need time alone after intimate moments to reflect and recharge. Share this need for space with your partner, so they understand that it's not a reflection of them, but rather your way of staying emotionally healthy.

The Emotional Dynamics of Sexuality for HSPs

Sexuality, like intimacy, is not just a physical experience for you— it is an emotional and psychological one. Your sensitivity amplifies your physical sensations, but it also makes sex feel more emotionally charged. For some HSPs, the emotional depth of sex can feel overwhelming, while for others, it is a source of profound connection and joy.

The challenge for many HSPs lies in balancing the emotional and physical aspects of sex. For example, you might find that you feel deeply connected to your partner emotionally but struggle with physical sensations that are too intense or overstimulating. Alternatively, the physical act of sex may feel like a release for pent-up emotional energy, but the emotional intensity can also lead to vulnerability or exhaustion afterward.

It's important to approach sexuality in a way that **honors both your emotional needs** and your **physical comfort**. Here are a few suggestions for navigating this balance:

1. Communicate Openly About Your Needs

Sexual experiences are deeply personal, and the more you communicate your needs and desires with your partner, the more fulfilling your sexual life will be. This includes discussing emotional aspects, such as the desire for intimacy or connection during sex, as well as physical preferences, such as pace, touch, or positioning.

It's important to be open with your partner about your needs for emotional security during sexual moments. If you need reassurance, comfort, or verbal affection, let your partner know. At the same time, encourage your partner to share their needs as well. Healthy communication will ensure that both emotional and physical needs are met.

2. Practice Sensuality Over Sexuality

For some HSPs, the term "sexuality" can feel overwhelming because of the intensity of physical sensations. If this resonates with you, consider embracing a more sensual approach to intimacy—one that emphasizes **touch**, **connection**, and **pleasure** without the pressure to have a certain type of sexual experience.

Sensual experiences can include activities like:
- **Slow dancing** or holding hands
- **Cuddling** and physical affection
- Taking **long, luxurious baths** together
- Sharing **quiet, intimate moments** like gazing into each other's eyes or sharing a meal

By focusing on sensuality, rather than on achieving a specific sexual outcome, you can cultivate a deeper emotional bond and enjoy intimacy without feeling overwhelmed by the expectations of sexual performance.

3. Respect Your Energy Levels

HSPs often experience **sensory overload** from the physical sensations associated with sex, especially if the experience is rushed, overly intense, or emotionally charged. It's important to listen to your body and recognize when your energy is depleted or when you need a break. There's no "one-size-fits-all" approach to intimacy, and it's perfectly okay to step back or take things at your own pace.

If sex is leaving you feeling drained, discuss it with your partner in a compassionate way. Share your needs and explore ways to make the experience more attuned to your emotional and physical sensitivities. By practicing self-awareness and respecting your own boundaries, you'll create a more harmonious sexual life that supports your well-being.

Conclusion: Embracing the Depth of Your Sexuality

Your emotional awareness is a **superpower** when it comes to intimacy and sexuality. It allows you to form deep, connected relationships where love, trust, and understanding flourish. By embracing your emotional sensitivity and practicing self-care, boundaries, and open communication, you can experience intimacy and sex in a way that nourishes your soul and honors your unique needs.

Remember that there is no right or wrong way to experience intimacy. Your sensitivity is a gift that enables you to connect with others on a profound level. By accepting and nurturing your emotional depth, you can transform your intimate relationships into sources of strength, joy, and mutual respect. Your emotional richness in sex and intimacy can lead to beautiful, fulfilling experiences—ones that empower you and your partner to experience love in its most authentic, vulnerable, and connected form.

Chapter 9:
Thriving in Work and Career: Leveraging Your Sensitivity for Success

As a Highly Sensitive Person (HSP), you approach your work and career with a level of care, depth, and attention to detail that many people admire. Your sensitivity allows you to pick up on nuances that others might miss—whether it's a subtle change in a colleague's tone, a potential flaw in a project, or an opportunity to improve a process. These abilities make you an incredibly valuable asset in the workplace, as you tend to produce high-quality work and cultivate harmonious working environments.

However, the very traits that make you an excellent worker can also pose challenges. The demands of the modern workplace—constant deadlines, high expectations, noisy environments, and emotional dynamics—can overwhelm your sensitive nervous system. This can lead to stress, burnout, and feelings of being misunderstood or unappreciated.

In this chapter, we will explore how to navigate the unique challenges of the work environment as an HSP while embracing your sensitivity as a **superpower**. By recognizing your strengths, setting boundaries, and fostering a work-life balance that nurtures your well-being, you can thrive in your career and create a path that honors your unique needs and aspirations.

The Superpower of Deep Focus and Attention to Detail

One of your greatest strengths as an HSP is your ability to focus deeply and work with meticulous attention to detail. Whether you are writing, designing, managing projects, or providing customer service, your ability to notice the subtleties and nuances in your work allows you to achieve results that are thorough and precise.

For example, in creative fields, you may have a unique talent for noticing small elements that others overlook—whether it's a slight inconsistency in a design or an underdeveloped character in a story. In analytical or technical fields, you can catch mistakes in calculations, identify patterns, or spot opportunities for improvement that others might miss. Your attention to detail helps ensure that your work is of the highest quality.

This sensitivity to detail is a superpower because it allows you to produce work that is not only accurate but also deeply impactful. While others may rush through tasks, your careful approach leads to a more polished and thoughtful final product. Your commitment to getting things right can build a reputation for you as a reliable and conscientious worker.

However, this same attention to detail can also cause you to overthink or get bogged down in perfectionism, especially when the stakes are high. To thrive in the workplace, it's important to recognize when your perfectionism is serving you and when it's hindering your progress.

Managing Sensory Overload in the Workplace

The modern workplace can be a sensory minefield for an HSP. Open offices, bright fluorescent lights, loud noise, constant emails, and a relentless pace of work can leave you feeling drained and overwhelmed. For many HSPs, sensory overload can lead to increased anxiety, irritability, and burnout, making it difficult to perform at your best.

Recognizing and managing sensory overload is essential to thriving in your career. Here are some practical strategies to help you cope:

1. Create a Quiet, Organized Workspace

If possible, design a workspace that minimizes sensory

distractions. This may include:
- Using **noise-canceling headphones** or playing soft, calming music to block out background noise.
- Organizing your desk and workspace in a way that reduces clutter and promotes focus.
- Choosing a workspace with natural light or using **adjustable lighting** to avoid harsh fluorescent lights.
- Setting up personal boundaries around your physical space, such as using a "do not disturb" sign during deep work.

Creating a calming environment can help you reduce sensory overload and improve your concentration, allowing you to perform your work at your best.

2. Take Regular Breaks and Practice Mindfulness

HSPs often need regular breaks throughout the day to recharge and reset. Overworking without breaks can lead to burnout and emotional exhaustion. Practice taking small breaks—whether it's a walk outside, deep breathing exercises, or even just a moment of stillness to clear your mind.

Additionally, practicing mindfulness throughout the day can help you stay grounded and reduce anxiety. Simple techniques like taking a few slow breaths, focusing on your senses, or doing a quick body scan can help calm your nervous system and bring your focus back to the present moment.

3. Limit Digital Overload

The constant barrage of emails, messages, and notifications can overwhelm your sensitive nervous system. Consider setting clear boundaries around digital communication:
- Turn off **non-essential notifications**.
- Schedule specific times to check your email or social media rather than checking constantly throughout the day.
- Use tools like "do not disturb" mode to limit distractions when you need to focus.

By taking control of your digital environment, you can reduce the sensory overload that often comes with constant connectivity and stay focused on your tasks.

Building Emotional Resilience in the Workplace

As an HSP, you feel deeply, and this emotional awareness can sometimes be a challenge in the workplace. You might find yourself affected by interpersonal dynamics, feeling empathetic toward colleagues in distress, or even internalizing negative feedback or criticism. These emotional responses can sometimes cause stress or lead to feelings of self-doubt.

Building emotional resilience is key to thriving in the workplace. Resilience doesn't mean suppressing your emotions, but rather learning how to manage and **protect** your emotional energy so that you can stay grounded, productive, and confident.

Here are some ways to build emotional resilience:

1. Practice Self-Compassion

When you face setbacks, criticism, or challenges in the workplace, be kind to yourself. HSPs often have a strong inner critic, which can amplify feelings of failure or inadequacy. However, self-compassion is essential to moving forward. Instead of being overly critical, treat yourself with understanding, just as you would offer support to a friend facing similar challenges.

Remind yourself that it's okay to make mistakes, to be imperfect, and to feel vulnerable. Your emotions are a natural part of your human experience, and treating yourself with compassion can help you bounce back from difficult moments with greater ease.

2. Seek Support and Mentorship

Emotional resilience also comes from having a strong support system. Seek out mentors or colleagues who understand your sensitivities and can offer guidance, reassurance, and practical advice. A supportive network can help you navigate difficult situations and offer a sense of belonging, which is crucial for emotional well-being.

Additionally, don't hesitate to seek professional support, such as therapy or coaching, to help manage workplace stress, perfectionism, or burnout. Having someone to talk to can help you gain perspective and develop strategies for coping with challenges.

3. Create Emotional Boundaries

As an HSP, you are highly attuned to the emotions of others, but it's essential to establish emotional boundaries. This means recognizing when you are absorbing the emotional energy of your colleagues and learning how to protect your emotional space. Setting boundaries allows you to care for others without becoming overwhelmed by their feelings.

For example, if a colleague is experiencing stress or frustration, you can offer empathy and support, but also recognize when you need to detach emotionally to maintain your own well-being. Learning to say "no" or stepping away from emotionally draining situations can help you conserve your emotional energy and remain balanced.

Aligning Work with Your Values and Purpose

One of the most fulfilling aspects of work for an HSP is aligning your career with your **values** and **purpose**. Because you feel deeply, you are likely to find the most satisfaction when your work reflects your core beliefs and contributes to something meaningful. You may be drawn to careers in helping professions, creative fields, social justice, or roles where you can make a tangible impact on others' lives.

If you feel unfulfilled in your current work, it may be helpful to reflect on how you can align your career more closely with your passions and values. Ask yourself questions such as:

- What activities make me feel most alive and engaged?
- How can I use my sensitivity to benefit others and create positive change?
- In what ways can my work contribute to a greater sense of purpose or fulfillment?

By identifying your values and integrating them into your work life, you will find greater joy and motivation in your career. Your sensitivity becomes a driving force for creating change, nurturing others, and contributing to the world in a meaningful way.

Conclusion: Thriving by Embracing Your Sensitivity

Your sensitivity is a **superpower** that enhances every aspect of your work life, from the quality of your output to your ability to connect with colleagues. While the modern workplace can present unique challenges for an HSP, by embracing your strengths and setting boundaries, you can thrive in your career.

Remember, success doesn't have to look like everyone else's. It's about creating a work environment that nurtures your well-being, supports your personal growth, and allows you to contribute to the world in a way that feels true to who you are. By recognizing and honoring your sensitivity, you can not only excel in your career but also build a path that leads to greater fulfillment, balance, and happiness.

Chapter 10:
Navigating Social Interactions: The Art of Connection for HSPs

As a Highly Sensitive Person (HSP), the way you experience social interactions is unlike most others. You have an extraordinary ability to tune into the emotions of those around you, to sense the unspoken dynamics in a room, and to absorb the subtle cues that guide human relationships. This gift allows you to build deep, authentic connections with others, but it can also make socializing overwhelming at times.

Whether it's a casual gathering, a large social event, or a one-on-one conversation, your sensitivity often leads you to feel deeply moved by the emotions, words, and energy of those around you. At its best, this sensitivity fosters empathy, understanding, and meaningful connections. At its most challenging, it can lead to overstimulation, social fatigue, or feelings of being misunderstood.

In this chapter, we will explore how to navigate social interactions as an HSP, understanding both the beauty and the challenges of your gift. By learning how to manage your social energy, set boundaries, and embrace your unique strengths, you can experience the joy of authentic connection while honoring your sensitive nature.

The Superpower of Empathy and Deep Connection

One of the most remarkable aspects of being an HSP is your innate **empathy**—the ability to sense and understand the emotions of others on a profound level. Whether you're in a group setting or one-on-one, you can often tell if someone is upset, excited, anxious, or joyful, even if they haven't said a word. This deep empathy enables you to form rich, meaningful relationships with those around you, as you are able to connect with others' emotional worlds in a way few can.

In social interactions, your ability to listen attentively and offer compassion makes others feel seen, heard, and understood. You are naturally inclined to offer support to friends, family, and even strangers who may need it, often intuitively knowing what they need—whether it's a comforting word, a helping hand, or simply someone to listen. These qualities can make you an invaluable friend, confidant, and companion.

However, your empathy can also be a double-edged sword. When you absorb too much of the emotional energy of others, especially in large groups or emotionally charged situations, you may find yourself overwhelmed, emotionally drained, or even anxious. Recognizing the delicate balance between offering empathy and preserving your own emotional energy is key to thriving socially.

Managing Overstimulation and Social Fatigue

Social situations, particularly those that involve large groups or unfamiliar environments, can be overwhelming for an HSP. The sensory input—conversations, background noise, body language, lighting, and the overall energy of the room—can quickly become too much, leaving you feeling drained and overstimulated. This social fatigue can manifest as irritability, anxiety, or the overwhelming desire to retreat and recharge.

To navigate these moments, it's essential to have strategies in place to protect your well-being and prevent burnout:

1. Set Realistic Expectations and Boundaries

Before heading into a social situation, take time to assess your emotional and physical needs. If you know that a gathering will be particularly stimulating or long, plan for ways to protect your

energy:
- **Set time limits**: Decide in advance how long you want to stay at the event. Giving yourself permission to leave early if you feel overwhelmed can help reduce anxiety.
- **Take breaks**: Step outside for a few minutes of fresh air or find a quiet space where you can recharge.
- **Know your triggers**: Be aware of situations that tend to overwhelm you—whether it's loud environments, intense conversations, or feeling crowded. By recognizing these triggers, you can take proactive steps to manage your energy.

2. Practice Grounding Techniques

When you begin to feel overstimulated or anxious in social settings, grounding techniques can help you stay centered and calm. These practices reconnect you to the present moment and can quickly shift your emotional state. Try:
- **Deep breathing**: Inhale slowly for four counts, hold for four, and exhale for four. This simple breathing pattern can help calm your nervous system.
- **Body awareness**: Pay attention to the sensation of your feet on the ground or the texture of an object in your hand. This helps you stay present and reduces the impact of overwhelming stimuli.
- **Mindful presence**: Rather than focusing on the noise or chaos around you, bring your attention back to the conversation or the moment at hand. Let go of distractions and focus on the connection.

By incorporating these grounding techniques, you can regain control of your energy and emotions, allowing you to continue engaging socially in a way that feels manageable.

Navigating Small Talk: Finding Authenticity in Casual Interactions

For many HSPs, small talk—the casual, surface-level conversations that often dominate social gatherings—can feel draining and inauthentic. You long for deeper, more meaningful conversations that allow you to truly connect with others. The banter about the weather, sports, or the latest trends can feel trivial, and you might find yourself mentally exhausted from trying to engage in these interactions.

But small talk doesn't have to be all bad. While it may not always be deeply fulfilling, small talk serves an important social function—it creates a foundation for connection and helps build rapport. If you can learn to approach it in a way that feels authentic, you can make even these seemingly shallow exchanges more enjoyable and meaningful.

1. Shift Your Focus to Active Listening

Rather than forcing yourself to contribute to every topic, try focusing on being a great listener. Active listening—paying full attention to the speaker, reflecting back what you hear, and asking thoughtful questions—can help you find meaning in the conversation without feeling overwhelmed. This approach also helps you avoid the pressure to perform or entertain.

By being present and engaged, you invite the other person to open up and share more deeply. Small talk can then evolve into more substantive conversations, allowing you to form genuine connections.

2. Ask Meaningful Questions

If you're craving more depth in your interactions, steer the conversation toward topics that resonate with you. Instead of the usual pleasantries, ask people about their passions, values, and experiences. Questions like:
- "What's been the most fulfilling part of your year so far?"
- "What project are you most excited about right now?"
- "What's something you've always wanted to learn or try?"

These types of questions invite a deeper connection and help steer the conversation toward authenticity.

Building Strong, Supportive Relationships

As an HSP, you tend to form deep, meaningful relationships with those you feel truly connected to. These are the relationships where you feel safe to be your authentic self, where vulnerability is met with understanding, and where emotional support flows freely.

However, as someone who experiences emotions intensely, navigating relationships can also be challenging. It's important to surround yourself with people who respect your sensitivities, honor your boundaries, and share your values.

1. Communicate Your Needs and Boundaries

In any relationship, clear and open communication is essential. As an HSP, it's especially important to share your needs, whether that's time alone to recharge, emotional support during stressful moments, or understanding if you need to leave an event early due to overstimulation.

When you communicate your needs kindly and confidently, it not only helps protect your energy but also fosters healthier, more understanding relationships. Most people will be grateful for the clarity and will be eager to support you in maintaining a balance between connection and self-care.

2. Seek Out Like-Minded Individuals

Building a strong social circle is about quality, not quantity. Surround yourself with people who understand and appreciate your sensitivities—those who can listen without judgment, offer emotional support, and respect your need for space when necessary.

You may find that you connect best with people who are also sensitive or who have a deep understanding of empathy. These relationships are often the most nurturing and energizing, allowing you to flourish socially without feeling overwhelmed.

Conclusion: Embracing the Art of Connection

As an HSP, your capacity for empathy, deep emotional connection, and authenticity makes you an extraordinary friend, partner, and colleague. Social interactions, while sometimes challenging, are an opportunity for you to use your sensitivity as a bridge to create deeper, more meaningful relationships with those around you.

By embracing your needs, setting healthy boundaries, and prioritizing self-care, you can navigate social settings with confidence and joy. Remember, the world needs your deep awareness and your ability to connect on a profound level. When you allow yourself to thrive socially—without overwhelming yourself—you create the space to form relationships that nourish your soul and honor your unique qualities.

Your sensitivity is not a barrier to connection; it's the key to building the kind of relationships that are rich, authentic, and deeply fulfilling.

Chapter 11:
Harnessing Your Sensitivity for Personal Growth and Transformation

Being a Highly Sensitive Person (HSP) means you are wired to experience life on a deeper, more nuanced level. You have an innate ability to perceive and process emotions, thoughts, and sensations in a way that many others cannot. While this can sometimes feel overwhelming, it also offers profound opportunities for **personal growth** and **transformation**.

Your sensitivity is not just something you navigate—it's a powerful tool for self-awareness, introspection, and emotional evolution. When you learn to work with your sensitivity instead of against it, it can lead you to greater emotional maturity, personal insight, and a deep sense of fulfillment.

In this chapter, we will explore how to embrace your HSP traits as pathways to personal growth. From cultivating emotional intelligence to finding your purpose, this chapter will show you how your sensitivity can become a transformative force in your life.

The Superpower of Emotional Awareness

At the core of being an HSP is a heightened sense of emotional awareness. You feel things more deeply than most, and this ability to tap into your emotions gives you the gift of **self-awareness**. Understanding your own emotional landscape is one of the most powerful tools you have for personal growth. When you are in tune with your emotions, you can gain clarity about what you need, what you value, and how you want to move forward in your life.

This emotional awareness also enables you to identify patterns in your life—whether it's the way you respond to certain people, how you deal with stress, or how you react to difficult situations. By becoming aware of these patterns, you can make more conscious choices that support your well-being and personal development.

1. Practice Emotional Reflection

Take time regularly to check in with yourself. Reflect on your emotional state and try to identify the underlying causes of your feelings. Journaling can be a powerful tool for this kind of reflection. By writing down your thoughts and emotions, you can gain clarity and better understand the root causes of your feelings.

For example, if you feel drained after a social event, ask yourself:
- Was it the people or the environment that overwhelmed me?
- Was I giving too much of my energy to others?
- Did I have enough time to recharge afterward?

Answering these questions can help you identify patterns and make adjustments in your life that support your emotional health. Self-reflection will also allow you to recognize when you're on the path to burnout or when you're thriving.

2. Use Your Emotional Intelligence for Growth

Your heightened emotional sensitivity is not just about recognizing your own feelings but also about understanding the emotions of others. This makes you especially attuned to the dynamics of relationships and can be a powerful tool for growth.

Emotional intelligence (EQ)—the ability to understand, use, and manage your emotions—is a vital skill for both personal and professional success. As an HSP, you are naturally inclined toward high emotional intelligence, and you can hone this ability

further through intentional practice:
- **Self-regulation**: Learn how to manage your emotions so that you don't become overwhelmed or overly reactive in difficult situations.
- **Empathy**: Continue to develop your ability to empathize with others while also setting boundaries to protect your energy.
- **Social skills**: Use your emotional insights to build stronger, more supportive relationships. As you grow in your emotional intelligence, you'll become more adept at communicating your needs and connecting with others on a deeper level.

Transforming Sensitivity into Strength: Overcoming Self-Doubt

As an HSP, you may occasionally struggle with self-doubt or feel misunderstood, particularly in environments that don't value your sensitivity. It's easy to feel as though your sensitivity is a burden or a weakness, especially if you're surrounded by people who don't understand your deep emotional responses or need for space. But the truth is, your sensitivity is one of your greatest strengths.

In fact, **sensitivity is often linked to creativity, intuition, and resilience**. It is a gift that allows you to be more in tune with yourself, more empathetic toward others, and more capable of finding meaningful solutions to challenges. When you begin to see your sensitivity as a strength, you unlock new possibilities for growth.

1. Reframe Your Sensitivity

Start by reframing how you view your sensitivity. Instead of seeing it as something to hide or control, see it as a powerful tool that enhances your life. When you embrace your sensitivity as an asset, you'll feel more empowered to navigate the world with confidence and authenticity.

Try these reframing techniques:
- **See emotional depth as a gift**: Recognize that your ability to

feel deeply allows you to experience life with richness and meaning.

- **Recognize your intuition as a guiding force**: Your gut feelings are often spot-on because your heightened senses pick up on things that others might miss. Trust your instincts.

- **Value your capacity for empathy**: Your ability to connect with others on an emotional level is an incredible gift. It enables you to create deep, supportive relationships and offer comfort to those in need.

When you begin to view your sensitivity as a source of power rather than vulnerability, you open the door to a more fulfilling and transformative life.

Setting Boundaries: Protecting Your Energy for Growth

One of the most important skills for any HSP on a path of personal growth is learning to **set healthy boundaries**. Boundaries are essential for maintaining emotional and physical well-being, especially when you're highly attuned to the needs and feelings of others. Without clear boundaries, you risk becoming drained, overwhelmed, and disconnected from your true self.

Setting boundaries allows you to prioritize your own needs while still offering empathy and support to others. When you set boundaries with compassion and clarity, you give yourself the space to thrive, without feeling depleted.

1. Identify Your Needs and Limits

Before you can set boundaries, you need to understand your own needs and limits. Take time to reflect on what makes you feel safe, supported, and energized. Are you someone who needs time alone to recharge after socializing? Do you need clear instructions and structure to feel focused at work? Do you thrive in calm, quiet environments or feel overwhelmed by noise and chaos?

Once you have a clearer understanding of your needs, you can begin to communicate them to others in a way that honors both your well-being and your relationships. When you articulate your boundaries, do so with kindness and confidence, knowing that you are protecting your own energy in order to show up as your best self.

2. Practice Saying No

As an HSP, you may have a tendency to overcommit or say yes to requests out of a desire to please others. However, overextending yourself can lead to burnout and resentment. Practice saying "no" when something doesn't align with your needs or values. Saying no doesn't make you selfish—it makes you self-aware and responsible for your own well-being.

Remember that you don't need to offer an elaborate explanation for your boundaries. A simple, polite "I can't take that on right now" or "I need some time for myself" is enough. Setting these limits not only helps you protect your energy but also models healthy boundaries for those around you.

Finding Your Purpose: Living Authentically

For many HSPs, finding and living in alignment with your **purpose** is a key aspect of personal growth. Because you feel so deeply and are so attuned to the world around you, you may be especially sensitive to a sense of calling or a desire to contribute meaningfully to the world. Whether it's through your work, relationships, creative endeavors, or acts of service, you have the potential to make a significant impact on the world when you align your actions with your values.

1. Listen to Your Inner Calling

Your sensitivity is a tool for understanding what truly matters to you. Listen closely to the things that stir your heart, inspire your creativity, or ignite your passions. These are clues that point you toward your purpose. Whether it's a deep desire to help others, a drive to create something beautiful, or an urge to make a difference in the world, your sensitivity guides you toward what feels most authentic.

2. Take Aligned Action

Once you have a sense of your purpose, take small steps to align your life with it. Don't feel pressured to have it all figured out at once—purpose is a journey, not a destination. Trust that your sensitivity will guide you toward the right path, and know that each step you take brings you closer to living authentically and with intention.

Whether you choose to pursue a new career, engage in creative projects, volunteer, or simply live in a way that aligns with your values, the key is to stay connected to your inner self and your deep sense of purpose.

Conclusion: Transforming Sensitivity into a Life of Fulfillment

Your sensitivity is not a flaw or something to be fixed. It is a profound gift that, when embraced, can lead you to a life of deep self-awareness, personal growth, and transformation. By cultivating emotional intelligence, setting boundaries, and aligning your actions with your values, you can create a life that is both fulfilling and authentic.

Remember, growth is a continuous process. Be patient with yourself as you navigate the path of self-discovery. With each step, you will uncover more of your potential and unlock new opportunities for growth, love, and purpose. Embrace your sensitivity, for it is not a hindrance—it is the key to living a life that is true to who you are.

Chapter 12:
The Impact of Sensitivity on Parenting

Parenting is often described as one of life's most transformative experiences, one that brings unparalleled joy but also unique challenges. For Highly Sensitive People (HSPs), the journey of parenting can feel both rewarding and overwhelming. This chapter delves into the dynamics of HSP parents raising children, particularly other HSP children, and explores strategies that can help these parents navigate the demands of family life while honoring their own needs.

HSP Parents Raising HSP Children

When an HSP parent discovers their child may also be highly sensitive, there's often a mix of emotions. They may feel an immediate connection and deep understanding of their child's emotional world, knowing firsthand the beauty and complexity of heightened sensitivity. Yet, they may also worry about the difficulties their child could face—a world that doesn't always accommodate deep feelers and gentle souls.

Understanding the Needs of an HSP Child
Highly sensitive children (HSCs) thrive when they feel safe, understood, and supported in their unique way of processing the world. Unlike many of their peers, HSCs can feel easily overwhelmed by loud noises, bright lights, or chaotic environments. They might withdraw from situations that others find stimulating or enjoyable, such as large birthday parties or crowded playgrounds. And when they feel misunderstood or criticized, they can internalize that hurt deeply, carrying it with them long after others have forgotten.

For HSP parents, recognizing and understanding these needs can come naturally. They can intuitively sense when their child is feeling overstimulated or needs a break. Unlike non-HSP parents who may view a child's sensitivities as a need for "toughening up," HSP parents are more likely to nurture their child's comfort levels and create an environment that honors their boundaries. The quiet strength and empathy of HSP parents become their superpower, allowing them to build a home that feels like a sanctuary.

The Gift of Empathy in Child-Rearing

An HSP parent's natural empathy can be one of their greatest assets. When a child has a meltdown after a long day at school, an HSP parent is often able to empathize rather than simply react. They can validate their child's feelings, saying, "I know today was hard for you, and it's okay to feel upset." This kind of response helps sensitive children feel safe and understood, which in turn builds their emotional resilience.

However, empathy can also be exhausting. HSP parents can find themselves absorbing their child's emotions so deeply that they begin to experience them as their own. The need to be constantly attuned, especially in the face of tantrums, tears, or sadness, can lead to emotional burnout. Yet, with mindfulness and a few strategies for managing their own boundaries, HSP parents can find ways to protect their own emotional well-being while remaining a steady, compassionate presence for their child.

Parenting Strategies for HSP Parents

Balancing the demands of parenting with the needs of a sensitive temperament can be challenging, but with some intentional adjustments, HSP parents can thrive. These strategies can help HSP parents not only create a balanced family life but also instill in their children the resilience, confidence, and emotional intelligence needed to navigate the world.

Balancing Your Needs with the Demands of Parenting

Parenting doesn't leave a lot of room for rest, particularly when children are young and require constant attention. For HSP parents, the ongoing demands can be draining. It's crucial for HSPs to recognize when they need to step back and recharge. Making time for solitude—even if it's just fifteen minutes in the morning or a quiet moment in the evening—can help HSP parents stay grounded and better able to meet the needs of their children.

Establishing a self-care routine can be invaluable. Whether it's journaling, meditating, or taking a daily walk, prioritizing personal well-being is essential. HSP parents should also feel empowered to ask for help when they need it. Family members, friends, and even childcare providers can step in to give them the break that's often essential for them to recharge. Embracing a flexible mindset, where self-care and parenting both have space, helps HSPs avoid burnout and approach each day with a renewed sense of patience and presence.

Creating a Nurturing, Sensory-Friendly Home Environment
Home is where an HSP and HSC alike can recharge and feel safe. For an HSP parent, crafting a home that minimizes stressors and encourages calm can make a world of difference. This might involve simple adjustments: soft lighting, cozy nooks for reading or resting, calming colors, and a general avoidance of overstimulating sounds or smells. These changes can transform the atmosphere of the home, creating a sanctuary that allows both parent and child to thrive.

Routines can also bring a comforting rhythm to daily life. Sensitive children often feel more secure when they know what to expect. Predictable routines around meals, bedtime, and transitions help alleviate stress, and by creating a structure that's gentle and flexible, HSP parents can provide their children with the stability they need without imposing rigid rules. In a home environment like this, sensitive children learn to self-soothe, express themselves freely, and explore the world at their own pace.

Embracing the Joy and Depth of Sensitive Parenting

Being a highly sensitive parent is a gift. It's a type of parenting that honors emotions, validates experiences, and fosters a compassionate, gentle bond between parent and child. The challenges may feel more intense, but the rewards are often profound: a deeper understanding of one another, a home that feels truly safe, and a shared journey of growing into one's own unique self.

In embracing their sensitivity, HSP parents offer their children a powerful message—that it's okay to feel deeply, to move through life gently, and to find strength in sensitivity.

Chapter 13:
Sensitivity and Boundaries: Protecting Your Energy

For Highly Sensitive People, maintaining healthy boundaries is essential yet challenging. With a natural inclination to care deeply and a heightened awareness of others' emotions, HSPs often find themselves stretched thin—emotionally, mentally, and even physically. This chapter explores the importance of boundaries for HSPs, offering insights and practical techniques for setting limits that honor their well-being while preserving their relationships.

How HSPs Can Set Healthy Boundaries

Understanding the Importance of Boundaries

Boundaries are not walls; they're invisible lines that help us protect our inner resources—our energy, focus, and emotional reserves. For HSPs, setting boundaries is not about shutting others out but about creating a balanced way to engage with the world. Without clear boundaries, HSPs can feel overwhelmed by others' demands, lose touch with their own needs, and experience burnout.

In relationships, healthy boundaries help HSPs preserve their own sense of identity. They create a space for both closeness and independence, allowing an HSP to engage fully while retaining their inner peace. In the workplace, boundaries help HSPs manage their workload, protect their creativity, and prevent emotional fatigue from overextending themselves. Setting and maintaining these boundaries is a form of self-respect, sending a message to others that their time and energy are valuable.

The Science of Emotional and Physical Energy Management

Research suggests that sensitivity can increase one's susceptibility to stress and overstimulation. HSPs experience heightened neural activity in response to both positive and negative stimuli, which can lead to a quicker depletion of their energy stores. Understanding this makes it clear why boundaries are essential: they're a means of managing the energy that HSPs have available each day.

Energy is like a resource, and for HSPs, even social interactions or work demands can quickly deplete it. Protecting this energy through boundaries allows HSPs to choose how they spend their time and with whom, helping them avoid overcommitment and retain a balanced, grounded presence.

Practical Techniques for Setting Boundaries

Scripts and Strategies for Assertive Communication

Setting boundaries can be intimidating for anyone, but HSPs may feel a particular reluctance, worried about causing disappointment or tension. The key lies in gentle but assertive communication— expressing needs clearly without apology. Here are some scripts and approaches designed to make boundary-setting feel respectful and compassionate:

1. **"I" Statements:** Using "I" statements frames boundaries in a way that doesn't blame the other person. For example, saying, "I need time each evening to recharge, so I'll be logging off at 6 p.m.," is a clear boundary without any accusation or defensiveness.

2. **Limiting Availability**: HSPs can feel pressured to respond immediately to messages or requests, especially at work. Try phrases like, "I'll need some time to think this over," or, "I can get back to you by tomorrow." These statements buy time, allowing you to manage your energy and avoid making decisions in haste.

3. **Saying No with Warmth**: Saying no can be hard, but framing it kindly can make it easier. A gentle, "I'd love to help, but I won't be able to this time," or, "I'm sorry, but my schedule won't allow it," can set a boundary without creating conflict. This approach validates the request while remaining firm.

4. **Setting Limits Around Emotional Labor**: In relationships, HSPs often find themselves as emotional "anchors." To set limits around this, try saying, "I care deeply about what you're going through, and I want to support you, but I need to take some time for myself, too." This approach communicates empathy while protecting your emotional energy.

Dealing with Boundary Pushback Compassionately
When setting boundaries, it's not uncommon to encounter resistance. For HSPs, who naturally feel empathy and a desire for harmony, boundary pushback can be particularly challenging. Here's how to handle it with compassion:

1. **Reaffirm Your Boundary Gently but Firmly**: If someone tries to push your boundary, you can kindly but confidently repeat your stance. For instance, "I understand you'd like me to attend, but I won't be able to make it." Reinforcing your boundary helps the other person understand that it's non-negotiable.

2. **Empathize Without Compromising**: Acknowledge the other person's feelings to soften the response. Try, "I can see this is important to you, and I appreciate your understanding that this is what I need right now." This affirms the relationship while holding your ground.

3. **Allow Space for Discomfort**: Some people may struggle with your boundary initially, but that doesn't mean it's wrong. Giving them space to adjust without rushing to make amends can be an act of respect for both parties. HSPs can find comfort in knowing that short-term discomfort often leads to long-term healthier relationships.

4. Reframe Guilt as Self-Care: When an HSP feels guilt for setting a boundary, it can help to reframe it as an essential part of self-care. Remind yourself that honoring your needs enables you to be present and engaged with others in a genuine way.

Creating a Lifestyle That Honors Boundaries

For HSPs, boundaries are not just a skill but a practice that evolves with life's demands and circumstances. Building a lifestyle that consistently honors boundaries can make the process feel more natural and rewarding. Here are a few ways to embed boundaries into everyday life:

1. **Routines that Center Your Well-being**: Establish routines that ground you—whether it's quiet time in the morning, a designated break after social engagements, or setting a strict cutoff time for work. These routines act as built-in boundaries that help sustain your energy.

2. **Evaluate Relationships Regularly**: Take time to assess your relationships and how they affect you. Relationships should be reciprocal and nourishing. When they're consistently draining, it's often a sign to re-establish or strengthen boundaries, preserving your energy for connections that bring joy and mutual respect.

3. **Check in with Yourself Daily**: Boundary-setting requires self-awareness, so cultivate a habit of daily check-ins. Ask yourself, "How am I feeling?" and "What do I need?" Pausing to tune into your own emotions allows you to address energy drainers early and adapt boundaries as needed.

Boundaries as a Path to Thriving

For Highly Sensitive People, boundaries are more than self-protection; they're a doorway to thriving. By honoring their sensitivity with boundaries, HSPs can lead a life that feels balanced and fulfilling, allowing them to show up wholeheartedly for the people and passions that matter most.

In embracing boundaries, HSPs give themselves permission to fully inhabit their lives, building resilience, fostering stronger connections, and nurturing the kind of inner peace that only comes from knowing—and respecting—their own worth.

Chapter 14:
HSPs and Social Interactions

For Highly Sensitive People, social interactions can be complex terrain. They bring opportunities for connection, understanding, and shared joy but can also lead to overstimulation, energy drain, and even a sense of disconnection if the HSP feels misunderstood or unseen. This chapter explores the nuances of social interactions for HSPs, with strategies for managing social energy and building fulfilling relationships that honor their sensitive nature.

Social Energy Management

Why Socializing Can Be Draining for HSPs
Social interactions, especially in larger groups or noisy environments, can be overwhelming for HSPs. With a heightened sensitivity to external stimuli, an HSP's nervous system can become easily overstimulated, leaving them feeling drained or mentally fatigued after events that might energize others. From the background noise in a crowded room to the subtle emotional cues others might miss, HSPs absorb and process a wealth of sensory and emotional information in social settings.

For many HSPs, this heightened sensitivity can create an inner conflict: they often crave connection and meaningful relationships but may feel that socializing comes at a high energetic cost. After spending time with friends or family, they may need quiet time to recharge and process. This doesn't mean HSPs don't enjoy socializing, but rather that they need to approach it with mindfulness to avoid emotional and physical burnout.

The Research on Introversion, Social Anxiety, and HSP Needs
Sensitivity and introversion often overlap, though not all HSPs are introverts. Studies show that around 70% of HSPs identify as introverted, while the remaining 30% may be more outgoing or ambiverted. Understanding whether one's need to withdraw is due to introversion or the unique requirements of being an HSP can be freeing—it allows HSPs to approach social situations in a way that aligns with their temperament rather than following social expectations.

Social anxiety, another common experience for some HSPs, may stem from a heightened awareness of others' emotional states or from past experiences of feeling misunderstood. While social anxiety can add layers of complexity, it's distinct from sensitivity itself. Many HSPs who do not experience social anxiety may still need to manage their energy carefully. A key to successful social interactions lies in understanding one's limits and recognizing that they don't reflect a lack of interest or connection but rather the unique way in which HSPs process their surroundings.

Tips for Managing Energy During Interactions
For HSPs, managing energy in social situations requires balance, self-awareness, and sometimes a few exit strategies. Here are some approaches to help HSPs protect their energy while still enjoying connections:

1. **Limit Social Commitments:** Consider the balance of social and alone time, planning activities that leave room for rest afterward. Declining a social invitation or suggesting a quieter venue isn't selfish—it's self-care.

2. **Set Time Limits:** If attending a social gathering, give yourself permission to set a time limit. You might say, "I'll come for an hour or so," which allows you to leave when you need to, avoiding the pressure to stay longer than you feel comfortable.

3. **Choose the Environment Carefully**: When possible, opt for places where the sensory load will be lower, such as a quiet cafe rather than a bustling restaurant or an outdoor park rather than a crowded bar. These environments can help HSPs feel more at ease and less overstimulated.

4. **Take Breaks**: During longer events, step outside or take a few moments to yourself to reset. A short walk, deep breaths, or even a few moments in a quiet room can do wonders to recharge.

5. **Engage in Meaningful Conversations:** HSPs often thrive in one-on-one or small group settings where conversations can go deeper. Seeking meaningful discussions over surface-level chit-chat can make interactions feel more fulfilling and less draining.

Building Healthy Social Networks

How to Find and Cultivate Friendships That Support Your Sensitivity

For HSPs, social interactions are often most fulfilling when they are based on genuine understanding, acceptance, and mutual respect. Finding people who understand the needs of a sensitive temperament isn't always easy, but cultivating friendships that support your sensitivity is worth the effort. Friendships that nourish rather than drain are built on empathy, shared values, and an understanding of each other's boundaries.

1. **Seek Like-Minded Individuals:** Joining groups or activities centered on interests that resonate with you—whether it's a book club, a creative workshop, or a nature group—can lead to friendships with people who value similar things and may even share your sensitivity.

2. **Be Open About Your Needs:** While it can feel vulnerable, sharing your need for quiet time or personal space with close friends can create an atmosphere of trust and respect. True friends will understand that your boundaries are not a reflection of the friendship's value, but rather a way to nurture it.

3. **Focus on Quality Over Quantity:** Many HSPs prefer fewer, deeper friendships to a wide social circle. Nurturing a smaller number of close relationships allows you to invest more meaningfully in each connection and reduces the likelihood of feeling overwhelmed.

4. **Respect Your Intuition**: HSPs often have a strong sense of intuition about people. Trusting these instincts can help in recognizing connections that feel safe and rewarding, avoiding relationships that may feel draining or one-sided.

The Role of Empathy in Social Bonding and Building Trust
One of the beautiful gifts that HSPs bring to relationships is empathy. Their natural ability to understand and tune into others' feelings fosters deep connections. This empathy allows HSPs to offer compassionate listening and authentic support, which can be transformative for their friends and loved ones. However, while empathy is a strength, it also requires balance to ensure HSPs don't absorb others' emotions to their own detriment.

Building Trust Through Boundaries and Reciprocity
Empathy and trust go hand in hand. For an HSP, feeling safe and valued in a friendship creates the foundation for authentic connection. Trust is built through consistent respect for each other's boundaries and a sense of reciprocity—where each person is both giving and receiving. When friendships have a balance of energy, HSPs can feel confident that their needs are being honored as much as they honor others'. Here are a few ways HSPs can foster trust and reciprocity:

1. **Communicate with Transparency:** Being honest about your feelings and needs, even when it's challenging, fosters trust. For example, letting a friend know when you need a break from social plans shows respect for the friendship and sets an example of open communication.

2. **Celebrate Differences:** Not all friends will understand sensitivity deeply, but respecting each other's differences can be a

powerful bonding tool. Allowing friends to be themselves while staying true to your needs reinforces the idea that friendship doesn't require sameness, only respect.

3. **Engage in Meaningful Reciprocity:** Look for friendships that have a balance of energy—where you can both listen and be heard. In supportive friendships, both people share their feelings, creating a space where HSPs can feel validated and valued for who they are.

Honoring Social Needs and Embracing Connection

For Highly Sensitive People, social interactions are enriched by a deep desire for authentic connection. By honoring their unique needs, HSPs can find ways to navigate social settings with confidence and ease. With energy management strategies and the right friendships, HSPs can create a fulfilling social life that doesn't compromise their inner peace.

Empathy, sensitivity, and authenticity are gifts that HSPs bring to every relationship, making their connections some of the most meaningful and supportive. In honoring their own boundaries and needs, HSPs give themselves permission to show up fully, creating relationships that feel safe, enriching, and genuinely nurturing.

Chapter 15:
Sensitivity and Personal Growth

For Highly Sensitive People, the journey of self-discovery and personal growth is often deeply enriched by their heightened sensitivity. This unique trait, which allows HSPs to feel emotions intensely and process experiences with profound depth, also serves as a powerful tool for transformation. In this chapter, we'll explore how sensitivity can be a guide toward self-awareness, healing, and a more purposeful life, as well as how it often enhances spiritual practices, providing a meaningful path toward inner peace and connection.

Using Sensitivity for Personal Transformation

The Power of Sensitivity for Self-Awareness, Growth, and Healing

HSPs possess a remarkable ability to turn inward and reflect on their thoughts, feelings, and experiences. This natural self-awareness provides a strong foundation for personal growth. With an intuitive understanding of their own emotions, HSPs can often identify what brings them joy, what triggers discomfort, and what they need to feel whole. This heightened awareness becomes a valuable guide on their journey, helping them make choices that are aligned with their true selves.

The ability to experience emotions so richly can sometimes feel overwhelming, but it's also a unique source of strength. Many HSPs find that through acknowledging and working with their emotions, they can move through life's challenges with greater resilience. Sensitivity encourages HSPs to pause, to observe their inner lives with compassion, and to find healing in moments of self-reflection.

Personal growth for an HSP often involves embracing their sensitivity as a gift rather than a burden. For example, by learning to honor their boundaries, HSPs discover the power of self-respect and self-care. By trusting their intuition, they strengthen their sense of confidence and authenticity. These experiences build a foundation of self-acceptance and allow them to step into the world feeling more empowered and whole.

How Emotional Depth Can Lead to a Greater Sense of Purpose

HSPs often feel a deep sense of purpose—a calling to make a meaningful contribution to the world or to live in a way that reflects their values. This desire is rooted in their emotional depth and empathy. Because HSPs tend to pick up on subtle details and underlying emotions, they are often more aware of issues, both personal and global, that may go unnoticed by others. This awareness can stir a powerful desire to bring healing, understanding, or beauty into the world.

Many HSPs find that their sensitivity connects them to causes they feel passionately about, such as the environment, human rights, or the arts. These pursuits not only provide an outlet for their compassion but also offer a way to channel their sensitivity into something that contributes positively to the world. Embracing their sensitivity as a guide toward purpose allows HSPs to engage in meaningful work that feels deeply fulfilling.

Another way HSPs find purpose is through personal relationships. By creating spaces where others feel safe, understood, and accepted, they make an impact on the lives of those around them. This role as an empathetic friend, parent, or partner often feels like a calling and can be just as powerful a form of purpose as a career or cause.

HSPs and Spirituality

How Heightened Sensitivity Can Deepen Spiritual Practices

For many HSPs, spirituality offers a sense of grounding,

belonging, and peace. Their natural inclination toward introspection, empathy, and a search for meaning often aligns with spiritual practices like mindfulness or prayer. In these practices, HSPs can find solace from the overstimulation of the external world and connect with a deeper part of themselves.

Meditation, for example, can be especially beneficial for HSPs. By focusing on the breath and quieting the mind, HSPs can learn to soothe their nervous systems, release emotional tension, and experience a profound sense of calm. In meditation, the sensitivity that sometimes feels overwhelming becomes a gift, allowing HSPs to experience each moment with clarity and depth. Similarly, mindfulness—a practice of being present and fully engaged with one's current experience—can help HSPs savor the small, beautiful details of life, creating a space for appreciation and gratitude.

HSPs who practice religion may find that their sensitivity allows them to connect with their faith in a very personal way. The stories, rituals, and symbols of their beliefs may resonate deeply, creating a sense of connection with something greater than themselves. This can be a source of strength and reassurance, especially in challenging times.

Research on the Spiritual Benefits of Being Highly Sensitive
Research on the link between sensitivity and spirituality suggests that HSPs often have a natural affinity for spiritual practices and experiences. Studies have shown that highly sensitive individuals are more likely to report a sense of awe in nature, a strong connection to music and art, and an interest in exploring questions of purpose and meaning. This inclination toward seeking the "bigger picture" may make spirituality a particularly rich area for HSPs.

One study found that HSPs were more likely to experience transcendent emotions—feelings of wonder, connection, and gratitude—which are often associated with spirituality. These experiences may not only bring a sense of peace and fulfillment but also contribute to the physical health of HSPs by lowering stress levels and improving emotional well-being. In this way, spirituality offers a pathway to both mental and physical health, helping HSPs manage their sensitivity in a way that promotes balance and resilience.

For HSPs, spirituality isn't just a practice; it can be a way of life, a source of guidance, and a place of refuge. By exploring this area of their lives, they may discover a wellspring of strength, comfort, and purpose that supports them in every other aspect of their journey.

Embracing Sensitivity as a Path to Transformation

For HSPs, sensitivity offers an extraordinary path to personal growth and spiritual connection. Through self-awareness, reflection, and compassion, HSPs can transform their sensitivity from a source of vulnerability into a wellspring of strength, healing, and purpose. By embracing practices that honor their depth, they can find ways to thrive, experiencing life's joys and challenges with resilience and peace.

In embracing spirituality, whether through organized religion, personal rituals, or a connection with nature, HSPs can discover a sense of belonging and meaning that transcends the everyday. Sensitivity, rather than being an obstacle, becomes a guide—one that leads them to their true self, their purpose, and a place of inner peace.

Chapter 16:
How HSPs Can Manage Conflict

Conflict can be especially challenging for Highly Sensitive People, as their heightened awareness of emotions and strong empathy often make them deeply affected by discord. However, these same qualities that make conflict difficult can also be their greatest strengths in resolving it. Sensitivity allows HSPs to approach disagreements with compassion, empathy, and an innate desire for understanding—all invaluable tools in conflict resolution. This chapter explores how HSPs can handle conflict in a way that not only reduces stress but also strengthens relationships, turning moments of tension into opportunities for growth and deeper connection.

Handling Conflict with Compassion

How HSPs Naturally Excel in Conflict Resolution Through Empathy and Deep Listening

HSPs have a natural ability to sense and understand the emotions of others. This empathy enables them to see conflicts not merely as battles of opposing opinions, but as situations where people's needs, fears, and desires are at play. By tuning into these underlying feelings, HSPs can approach conflict with compassion rather than defensiveness, making it easier to find common ground. Their willingness to truly listen—without judgment or immediate rebuttal—helps them understand others' perspectives, which is a powerful foundation for conflict resolution.

In tense situations, HSPs' deep listening skills can serve as a balm for others. Many people feel unheard or misunderstood in conflicts, which often fuels frustration and escalates disagreements. By creating a safe space where others feel seen and respected, HSPs can defuse some of the emotional charge in a disagreement, helping everyone involved feel more willing to find a solution.

Research on Conflict Management Styles and the Advantages of Sensitivity

Studies on conflict management suggest that different people approach conflict in unique ways, often falling into styles such as avoiding, accommodating, competing, compromising, or collaborating. HSPs often gravitate toward the "accommodating" or "collaborating" styles due to their empathy and desire to maintain harmony. While accommodating involves prioritizing others' needs over one's own, collaborating seeks to meet everyone's needs through open communication and problem-solving.

HSPs tend to excel at collaboration, often feeling most at ease when they can find solutions that honor all parties involved. Research shows that individuals who are more empathic are more successful in finding win-win solutions, as they're able to see and value multiple perspectives. By leaning into their natural inclination for collaboration, HSPs can turn potential points of conflict into opportunities for teamwork and mutual understanding.

HSPs may also find that when they handle conflicts with compassion and openness, others are more likely to respond in kind. This approach helps create a ripple effect, inspiring a more understanding and supportive response from others, which can be transformative in both personal and professional relationships.

Turning Conflict into Connection

How to Navigate Disagreements and Turn Them Into Opportunities for Deeper Understanding

For HSPs, conflicts are often painful but can also be deeply meaningful. When approached with openness and curiosity, disagreements can reveal important insights into each person's needs, values, and boundaries. Instead of viewing conflict as something to avoid or minimize, HSPs can use it as a chance to build trust and intimacy by exploring what truly matters to both parties.

Navigating disagreements with this mindset requires an attitude of non-judgment. For example, rather than seeing a partner's frustration as a personal attack, HSPs can try to view it as an expression of an unmet need or unaddressed concern. By asking gentle, clarifying questions like "What would help you feel more supported?" or "How can we work together to make this better for both of us?", HSPs can shift the conversation from defensiveness to cooperation.

Another key to turning conflict into connection is self-compassion. HSPs may have a tendency to take on others' emotions or feel responsible for resolving issues on their own. By practicing self-compassion—reminding themselves that they too deserve respect, kindness, and understanding—they can enter conflicts with a balanced perspective that respects both their own needs and those of others.

Effective Communication Strategies to Express Needs and Emotions

Effective communication is essential in conflict resolution, especially for HSPs who may feel deeply affected by disagreements. Here are several communication strategies tailored to HSPs that can help them express their needs and emotions with clarity and compassion:

1. **Use "I" Statements:** Instead of framing things in terms of what the other person has done, use "I" statements to express how you feel. For example, saying "I feel overwhelmed when there's a lot of noise" is more constructive than "You're always so loud." This approach minimizes defensiveness and focuses on your experience, helping others understand your perspective without feeling blamed.

2. **Acknowledge the Other Person's Feelings**: In conflict, simply acknowledging the other person's emotions can be transformative. Statements like, "I can see that you're really

passionate about this" or "I understand that this issue matters to you" can build rapport and make the other person feel seen. When people feel understood, they are more likely to reciprocate that understanding.

3. **Express Your Needs Without Apology**: HSPs sometimes hesitate to assert their needs, fearing they'll disrupt harmony or cause tension. However, expressing your needs is essential for a balanced relationship. Try framing your needs in a positive light, such as "I feel more comfortable discussing things in a calm setting" or "I need a little time to process this before we talk." This approach helps ensure that your needs are heard while maintaining respect for the other person's perspective.

4. **Practice Mindful Pausing**: In moments of heightened tension, taking a mindful pause can be powerful. Pausing allows HSPs to reconnect with their inner calm, preventing reactive responses. If you need a break, saying something like "I need a moment to gather my thoughts" or "Can we take a quick break and come back to this?" can help prevent misunderstandings and give both parties space to process.

5. **Set Boundaries on Overwhelming Topics**: Some conflicts can be particularly emotionally charged, and it's okay to set boundaries if certain discussions are too overwhelming. For example, if a conversation becomes too intense, an HSP might say, "This is important to me, but I think I need a bit of space right now. Let's revisit this soon." Setting limits on emotionally intense topics allows HSPs to protect their energy and approach the issue from a more balanced place.

Embracing Sensitivity as a Strength in Conflict

For HSPs, the idea of conflict can feel intimidating, but it's also an opportunity to bring their unique gifts of empathy, compassion, and insight into challenging situations. By handling conflict with sensitivity and openness, HSPs can create more harmonious, understanding, and authentic connections. Conflict doesn't have to be about "winning" or "losing"—it can be a journey toward understanding, where both sides feel heard, valued, and connected.

As HSPs learn to honor their own needs while respecting others, they can transform conflict into a source of growth and connection. Sensitivity becomes not a barrier to overcome but a bridge that brings people closer, creating relationships built on trust, respect, and mutual support. Through compassionate conflict resolution, HSPs not only protect their own well-being but also become catalysts for deeper, more meaningful connections in every area of their lives.

Chapter 17:
The HSP's Relationship with Technology

Technology has become an integral part of our lives, offering both incredible conveniences and unique challenges, especially for Highly Sensitive People. For HSPs, the constant stream of notifications, information, and digital interaction can quickly become overwhelming. Sensitivity heightens the impact of overstimulation, making it crucial for HSPs to be mindful about their technology use. In this chapter, we'll explore how the digital world affects HSPs and share strategies for creating a balanced, healthy relationship with technology.

The Effects of Technology on HSPs

How Screen Time, Social Media, and Constant Connectivity Affect HSPs

The digital age has introduced new forms of connection and information sharing that can be exciting but also overwhelming for HSPs. The very qualities that make technology so engaging—the endless news feeds, social media updates, and constant availability of information—can lead to sensory overload. HSPs, who are already highly attuned to stimuli, may find that prolonged screen time or extensive use of social media leaves them feeling drained, anxious, or overstimulated.

Social media, in particular, can have mixed effects on HSPs. On the positive side, it provides a way to connect with like-minded individuals, share ideas, and stay informed. For HSPs who value meaningful relationships and deep conversations, social platforms can offer a sense of community. However, social media can also become a source of stress due to its tendency to magnify comparison, criticism, and negativity. Scrolling through curated images of others' lives or encountering divisive opinions can be emotionally taxing for HSPs, who may absorb these feelings more intensely than others.

Similarly, the constant connectivity enabled by smartphones and other devices can disrupt HSPs' sense of peace. The pressure to respond immediately to messages or stay updated on every news alert can feel overwhelming, as HSPs are often more affected by the emotional implications of communication. The cumulative effect of all this digital input can lead to burnout, anxiety, or a general sense of "noise" in the mind.

Research on Overstimulation in the Digital Age
Research highlights the unique impact of digital overstimulation on mental health, and HSPs may be particularly vulnerable. Studies show that frequent screen time, especially on social media, is associated with increased stress, anxiety, and decreased overall well-being. Notifications and alerts create interruptions that can disrupt concentration and increase stress levels, leaving the mind in a state of heightened alertness. For HSPs, who process information deeply, these constant interruptions can contribute to mental fatigue, emotional exhaustion, and an increased risk of burnout.

One aspect of digital overstimulation is decision fatigue. Every interaction with technology—choosing which emails to read, deciding whether to reply to a message, selecting which news articles to open—requires a small decision. Over time, these choices add up, creating a sense of mental fatigue that can make it harder for HSPs to focus on what truly matters.

Creating a Healthy Tech Environment

Strategies for Reducing Tech Overwhelm (Digital Detox, Mindful Use of Technology)
To protect their well-being, HSPs can benefit from setting boundaries around technology use. A digital detox—temporarily reducing or eliminating screen time—can be a powerful reset, helping HSPs regain a sense of clarity and peace. Even a short break from screens, such as dedicating one day a week to being

device-free, can reduce feelings of overwhelm and give the mind a chance to relax.

Mindful use of technology is another effective approach. This involves being intentional about when, where, and how to engage with devices, rather than allowing screens to dictate one's time and attention. Here are some mindful technology practices that can support HSPs:

1. **Schedule Tech-Free Times**: Designate certain times of the day to be tech-free. For example, avoid screens during meals, in the first hour after waking, or before bed. These moments can help HSPs reconnect with the present moment, relax their minds, and recharge their energy.

2. **Curate Your Digital Environment**: Be selective about which apps, notifications, and content you allow into your digital life. For instance, consider unfollowing accounts that trigger stress or overwhelm, turning off non-essential notifications, or organizing apps so that only the most meaningful or useful ones are easily accessible. Creating a streamlined digital environment can reduce sensory input and make technology feel more manageable.

3. **Set Boundaries Around Social Media**: While social media can be a great way to stay connected, HSPs may benefit from limiting the amount of time spent on these platforms. For instance, consider setting daily time limits for social apps or unfollowing accounts that provoke negative emotions. Engaging mindfully and selectively on social media allows HSPs to enjoy the positive aspects of connection without becoming overwhelmed.

4. **Engage in Purpose-Driven Technology Use**: Before reaching for a device, take a moment to clarify your intention. Are you checking your phone out of habit, or do you have a specific purpose, like sending a message or researching information? Setting an intention helps create awareness, encouraging HSPs to use technology in a way that serves them rather than feeling controlled by it.

5. **Create Digital Breaks During Work**: If work requires prolonged screen time, take regular breaks to rest your eyes, stretch, or simply breathe deeply. HSPs might find that stepping away from their devices, even briefly, can prevent mental fatigue and enhance focus.

How to Balance Productivity with Mindful Tech Usage
For many HSPs, balancing the productivity benefits of technology with the need for peace and mindfulness is essential. Productivity tools, apps, and connectivity can be incredibly useful, allowing HSPs to work efficiently and stay organized. However, using these tools mindfully can prevent them from becoming a source of stress. Here are a few strategies to help HSPs balance productivity with mindful tech usage:

1. **Set Clear Work Hours and Log Off**: When working from home or on flexible schedules, HSPs can feel pressured to stay available. Setting clear work hours—and truly logging off when the workday ends—helps create separation between personal time and work time, allowing for rest and renewal.

2. **Use Technology to Enhance Organization, Not Overwhelm**: Choose a few essential productivity tools that genuinely support your needs without overloading you with reminders, notifications, or data. Tools that simplify rather than complicate, like a single calendar app or a minimal to-do list, can enhance productivity without creating overwhelm.

3. **Batch Notifications and Emails:** Rather than checking emails or messages constantly, try setting specific times to check them, such as once in the morning and once in the afternoon. This helps reduce the number of interruptions, making it easier to focus on tasks without feeling pulled in multiple directions.

4. **Prioritize Focus-Enhancing Apps and Settings:** Many devices offer features designed to minimize distractions, such as "Do Not Disturb" modes or focus timers. HSPs can use these tools to block distracting notifications during focused work periods or relaxation times, creating a tech environment that

supports their need for calm.

5. Incorporate Mindful Breaks into Tech Use: Rather than viewing breaks as an interruption to productivity, see them as a vital part of maintaining mental clarity and focus. HSPs who regularly take short, tech-free breaks are more likely to experience sustained energy and reduced stress over the course of the day.

Embracing a Healthy Relationship with Technology

For Highly Sensitive People, creating a balanced relationship with technology involves both awareness and intention. Technology offers remarkable tools for connection, learning, and productivity, but it's essential for HSPs to engage with it in ways that support their unique needs. By setting boundaries, practicing mindful tech habits, and curating their digital environment, HSPs can protect their energy and foster a sense of peace in the midst of the digital world.

Mindful use of technology allows HSPs to experience the benefits of connectivity while still honoring their sensitivity. By tuning in to what feels nourishing and aligning tech habits with their personal values, HSPs can navigate the digital age with confidence, calm, and balance. This approach transforms technology from a source of stress into a supportive tool, helping HSPs thrive in a way that feels both productive and deeply aligned with their well-being.

Chapter 18:
HSPs and Aging:
A Lifetime of Sensitivity

Growing older as a Highly Sensitive Person brings unique gifts and challenges, with sensitivity shaping each stage of life in profound ways. While sensitivity may have presented difficulties in youth, such as feeling "different" or overly affected by experiences, it often becomes a source of resilience, insight, and depth in later years. Many HSPs find that with age, their sensitivity becomes not only a cherished part of who they are but also a tool for creating meaningful connections, reflecting on life with a greater understanding, and embracing the beauty of each moment.

This chapter explores the ways sensitivity evolves over a lifetime, offering a compassionate look at the challenges and rewards of aging as an HSP. We'll also share ways to support mental, emotional, and physical well-being as Highly Sensitive People move through later stages of life, making the most of their capacity for reflection, empathy, and inner strength.

Sensitivity Across the Lifespan

How Sensitivity Changes with Age and Life Stages
Sensitivity is a stable trait that often remains with HSPs from childhood through older adulthood, yet the way it expresses itself can change over time. In youth, HSPs may be acutely affected by their environments, including school, social dynamics, and family life. The sensitivity to criticism, overstimulation, and complex emotions that many young HSPs feel can sometimes be overwhelming, especially in settings that don't encourage emotional expression or honor individual differences. Many HSPs remember their younger years as a time of heightened intensity and occasional isolation, where they often felt "different" or

misunderstood.

However, as HSPs grow older, they often develop a stronger sense of identity and learn coping strategies that make sensitivity easier to manage. Through life experiences, many HSPs become more self-assured, learning to value their unique perspectives rather than feeling "too sensitive" or "out of place." The emotional depth and empathy that may have felt burdensome in youth often evolve into sources of wisdom and compassion, helping HSPs connect with others on a deep level.

Research on emotional regulation suggests that, with age, many people develop a stronger ability to manage their emotions. For HSPs, this can mean that as they grow older, they become more adept at handling stress and more intentional about creating environments that support their well-being. Sensitivity becomes less about reacting to external stimuli and more about savoring meaningful connections, finding joy in simple moments, and using intuition and empathy to make thoughtful life choices.

The Long-Term Benefits of Being an HSP in Older Adulthood

In older adulthood, the gifts of sensitivity often come into full bloom. The deep sense of empathy, appreciation for beauty, and introspective nature that characterize HSPs contribute to a rich inner life that can make aging a deeply fulfilling experience. Many HSPs find that they are more resilient in the face of challenges, as their sensitivity allows them to process complex emotions, find meaning in life changes, and adapt to new circumstances with grace.

Research on aging and well-being suggests that the capacity for positive emotion often increases with age, with older adults tending to focus more on meaningful relationships, inner peace, and gratitude. HSPs, who are naturally inclined to seek depth and meaning, can find even greater joy and fulfillment as they embrace these values in their later years. Aging provides the chance to focus more on what truly matters—time with loved ones, creative pursuits, or moments of reflection in nature—all of which align with the HSP's intrinsic desire for depth and connection.

In addition, HSPs often become sources of wisdom and support within their communities and families, as their life experiences and empathetic nature allow them to offer guidance, understanding, and unconditional love. By sharing their perspectives and insights, older HSPs contribute to the emotional richness of their relationships, creating a legacy of compassion and understanding.

Adapting to Aging as an HSP

How to Support Mental, Emotional, and Physical Well-Being as an HSP Gets Older
Maintaining well-being as an HSP in older adulthood involves caring for the mind, body, and spirit. Here are several strategies to help HSPs thrive as they age:

1. **Prioritize Rest and Quiet**: As energy levels may change with age, creating a routine that includes time for rest and quiet reflection becomes even more essential. HSPs can benefit from structuring their days to include moments of calm, such as reading, meditating, or enjoying time in nature. These activities can help replenish energy and provide peace of mind.

2. **Engage in Meaningful Relationships**: HSPs often value close, supportive relationships that nurture their emotional needs. As they age, focusing on these meaningful connections—whether with friends, family, or community members—can enhance well-being and prevent feelings of isolation. Simple acts like sharing stories, reminiscing, or spending time with loved ones offer a sense of continuity, belonging, and purpose.

3. **Pursue Creative and Reflective Activities**: Creativity and introspection are often sources of joy for HSPs, and aging provides a wonderful opportunity to explore these interests. Whether it's painting, journaling, gardening, or engaging in other forms of self-expression, creative pursuits allow HSPs to channel

their sensitivity into something beautiful and fulfilling. Reflective practices, such as writing about life experiences or documenting family memories, can also create a sense of legacy and accomplishment.

4. **Cultivate a Positive Relationship with Physical Health**: Physical health plays a crucial role in emotional well-being, especially as we age. HSPs may be sensitive to their bodies' needs and can use this awareness to develop a health routine that includes gentle exercise, balanced nutrition, and mindful movement. Activities like walking, yoga, or tai chi can be especially beneficial for HSPs, providing both physical health benefits and a sense of inner peace.

5. **Manage Sensory Overload Mindfully**: Overstimulation may remain a challenge, especially in busy or noisy environments. HSPs can benefit from developing coping strategies, such as using noise-canceling headphones, practicing deep breathing exercises, or taking breaks during social gatherings to recharge. By respecting their sensory needs, HSPs can enjoy life's moments more fully without feeling overwhelmed.

The Advantages of Introspection and Reflection in Later Life
One of the greatest gifts of sensitivity in older adulthood is the capacity for introspection. HSPs have a natural ability to reflect deeply, often finding meaning and wisdom in their experiences. In later life, this introspective quality becomes even more valuable, offering a way to process and appreciate the journey of a lifetime.

Reflection provides a sense of continuity, helping HSPs see how each stage of life has contributed to their growth. Taking time to look back on experiences, challenges, and achievements can create a sense of closure and gratitude, allowing HSPs to approach the future with peace and contentment. Many HSPs find that reflection gives them a stronger sense of self, helping them feel more connected to their values, beliefs, and aspirations.

The quiet, reflective nature of aging also opens up new possibilities for spiritual exploration. Whether through meditation, prayer, or simply spending time in nature, HSPs can deepen their connection to themselves, their beliefs, or a greater sense of purpose. For many HSPs, this spiritual dimension of aging brings a profound sense of joy and wonder, allowing them to see beauty and meaning in life's simplest moments.

Embracing Sensitivity as a Lifelong Gift

As HSPs move through each stage of life, their sensitivity remains a unique gift, shaping how they experience the world and relate to others. Aging as an HSP means not only adapting to physical and emotional changes but also embracing the wisdom, empathy, and inner richness that come with a lifetime of sensitivity. Each decade brings new insights and opportunities, transforming sensitivity from a source of vulnerability into a wellspring of resilience, compassion, and understanding.

For HSPs, aging is an invitation to deepen their relationships, find joy in simple pleasures, and celebrate the beauty of a reflective, intentional life. With self-compassion, adaptability, and an open heart, Highly Sensitive People can look forward to a lifetime of growth, connection, and fulfillment. Sensitivity becomes a legacy that lives on not only in the memories they cherish but also in the love, wisdom, and understanding they offer to others. Aging, for HSPs, is not merely about getting older—it's about continuing to grow, love, and find meaning, honoring the journey in all its richness and depth.

Chapter 19:
Thriving as an HSP in a Non-HSP World

Being a Highly Sensitive Person in a world that often values speed, competition, and resilience can be both challenging and rewarding. HSPs are naturally empathetic, attuned to their surroundings, and sensitive to subtleties, which can lead to profound insights and connections. However, society doesn't always recognize or accommodate these strengths. In many environments—workplaces, schools, or even families—sensitivity can be misunderstood or undervalued, leaving HSPs feeling pressured to adapt to a world that seems at odds with their nature.

Despite these challenges, it's possible for HSPs to thrive by embracing their unique qualities, advocating for their needs, and finding or creating communities that value sensitivity. In this chapter, we'll explore how HSPs can navigate societal expectations, cope with misunderstanding, and build a supportive environment that allows them to flourish.

Living in a World that Doesn't Always Understand Sensitivity

The Societal Challenges HSPs Face

Highly Sensitive People often encounter unique challenges as they move through environments that may not be designed with sensitivity in mind. In the workplace, for example, HSPs might struggle in high-stress settings that emphasize constant multitasking, immediate responsiveness, and competitive mindsets. Open office plans, frequent meetings, or demanding workloads can quickly lead to overstimulation, making it harder for HSPs to perform at their best.

Schools, too, may pose difficulties. Traditional educational systems often prioritize speed, standardized testing, and extraverted participation, which can be overwhelming for sensitive children who might need more time to process information or prefer quiet reflection to group activities. As a result, sensitive students may feel misunderstood by teachers or peers, which can impact their confidence and academic performance.

Even within families, HSPs may experience misunderstanding or pressure to be more "resilient" or less "emotional." Family members who don't share the trait of sensitivity may interpret the HSP's needs as oversensitivity or weakness, which can lead to feelings of isolation or self-doubt. For children and adults alike, these experiences can create a sense of being "different" or somehow "less capable" than others, when in reality, HSPs simply thrive in environments that respect and nurture their unique qualities.

How to Cope with Criticism, Misunderstanding, and Societal Expectations
Learning to navigate criticism, misunderstanding, and societal expectations is essential for HSPs who want to feel empowered in their sensitivity rather than constrained by it. Here are some strategies to help HSPs cope with these challenges:

1. **Reframe Criticism as Insight**: Criticism can feel intensely personal to HSPs, but reframing it as feedback or insight can help create emotional distance. Ask yourself, "Is there a kernel of truth here that I can use for growth?" or "Does this criticism reflect the other person's perspective rather than my true self?" This reframing can turn criticism into a learning tool rather than a personal attack.

2. **Practice Self-Validation**: One of the most empowering practices for HSPs is self-validation. Instead of relying solely on external approval, remind yourself that your thoughts, feelings, and experiences are valid. Self-validation reinforces the idea that sensitivity is a strength, and that it's okay to have different needs

and preferences.

3. **Set Boundaries with Compassion**: Boundaries are essential in environments where sensitivity may be misunderstood. Politely yet assertively explaining your needs can help others understand your limits. For example, if you need alone time after work, gently let family members know that it helps you recharge and feel more present with them later.

4. **Find Meaning in Your Sensitivity**: Recognizing the gifts that come with sensitivity—such as empathy, creativity, and intuition—can help counterbalance societal expectations that may feel pressuring or critical. Remind yourself of times when your sensitivity has made a positive difference, whether through offering support to a friend, creating something beautiful, or making a thoughtful decision. This practice reinforces the value of sensitivity and helps you see it as a source of strength.

5. **Connect with Like-Minded Individuals**: Finding other HSPs or people who appreciate sensitivity can provide relief from societal pressures. Building friendships with those who understand your experiences or joining online communities for HSPs can offer validation and support, allowing you to feel connected to a larger, understanding community.

Empowering Yourself and Others

How to Advocate for Your Needs and Educate Others About HSPs

Advocacy is an empowering way for HSPs to honor their needs while fostering understanding in others. Speaking up about your sensitivity, in a thoughtful and clear way, helps people in your life recognize and appreciate your unique strengths. Here are some ways to effectively advocate for yourself and educate others:

1. **Share Your Perspective with Openness and Honesty**: Educating others about HSPs can often be as simple as sharing your experiences in a conversational way. For example, you might say, "I'm someone who tends to notice subtleties and feels things

deeply—it's part of being highly sensitive. It allows me to be very empathetic and intuitive, though it also means I sometimes need quiet time to recharge." Offering this kind of insight can help others see your sensitivity as a natural, valuable trait rather than something unusual or inconvenient.

2. **Frame Your Needs as Positive Self-Care**: When explaining your needs to others, it can be helpful to frame them in terms of positive self-care. For example, instead of saying, "I can't handle loud events," try, "I recharge best in quieter settings and would love to spend time in a way that allows us to really connect." This approach shifts the conversation from limitation to preference, making it easier for others to understand and respect your needs.

3. **Use Resources to Educate**: Many people still aren't familiar with the concept of high sensitivity, and sharing educational resources—such as books, articles, or videos—can help bridge the gap. You might offer a friend or colleague a link to an article on HSPs, saying, "This explains a lot about how I experience things. It's helped me understand myself better, and I thought it might help you understand why certain things matter to me."

4. **Stand Confidently in Your Sensitivity**: Often, the way we present our needs affects how others respond. If you confidently embrace and communicate your sensitivity, others are more likely to respect it. Know that your needs are valid and that advocating for them is an essential part of thriving as an HSP.

Building a Community of Support and Understanding for Sensitive Individuals

For HSPs, community is a key source of strength and empowerment. Finding people who appreciate and understand sensitivity creates a safe space for authentic expression and growth. Here are ways to build a supportive community that values and nurtures your sensitivity:

1. **Seek Out HSP Communities**: Many HSPs find support through online communities, local meetups, or support groups specifically designed for Highly Sensitive People. These spaces

provide an opportunity to share experiences, exchange advice, and celebrate the gifts of sensitivity. Connecting with others who face similar challenges and joys can be both validating and comforting.

2. **Foster Close, Trusting Relationships**: While HSPs may not seek large social networks, they often value deep, meaningful connections. Nurture relationships with people who appreciate your sensitivity, whether they are other HSPs or individuals who respect and value your unique qualities. Cultivating these connections provides emotional support and reinforces the value of sensitivity.

3. **Advocate for Sensitivity Awareness in Your Circles**: You can also help create a more HSP-friendly environment by advocating for sensitivity awareness in your workplace, school, or community. For example, if you're comfortable, you could suggest workplace practices like "quiet hours" or flexible scheduling options that benefit HSPs and others who work better with fewer interruptions. Educating those around you on the benefits of accommodating different needs can promote a more inclusive, understanding environment.

4. **Lead by Example**: Embracing and honoring your sensitivity can inspire others to do the same. By demonstrating self-compassion, setting boundaries, and confidently expressing your needs, you show others that sensitivity is a valuable trait. This quiet form of advocacy can encourage others to be more mindful, empathetic, and accepting of their own and others' differences.

Celebrating Sensitivity in a Non-HSP World

Living as a Highly Sensitive Person in a non-HSP world comes with unique challenges, but it also brings opportunities to grow, connect, and contribute in meaningful ways. While it may sometimes feel isolating to be sensitive in a world that doesn't always understand or accommodate it, remember that sensitivity is a profound strength, offering insights, compassion, and creativity that make the world a richer place.

By advocating for your needs, educating those around you, and building supportive relationships, you create an environment where sensitivity can thrive. And as you embrace your true self, you may find that others are inspired by your authenticity, leading to deeper connections and a more understanding world. Thriving as an HSP means not only accepting sensitivity as a fundamental part of who you are but also celebrating it as a gift that brings depth, kindness, and beauty to everything you touch.

Chapter 20:
Embracing Your Superpower

As we reach the end of this journey, it's time to step back and look at everything you've learned, experienced, and reflected upon. You've explored what it means to be a Highly Sensitive Person in a world that can sometimes feel overwhelming, yet also full of beauty, meaning, and opportunity. You've discovered that sensitivity isn't a trait to hide or "overcome"—it's a remarkable strength, a superpower that can bring deep, lasting value to your life and the lives of those around you.

In this final chapter, let's celebrate the gift of sensitivity, a quality that brings profound empathy, insight, and understanding into a world that truly needs it. We'll also guide you through creating a personal "HSP Superpower Blueprint"—a step-by-step approach to embrace your sensitivity and use it as a guiding force for a life well-lived. This chapter is a call to recognize, honor, and nurture your sensitivity, using it as a compass that can lead you to greater fulfillment, purpose, and joy.

How to Embrace Sensitivity as a Gift

Recognizing Sensitivity as a Source of Strength
Being highly sensitive comes with unique challenges, as you well know. But as you've likely discovered throughout this book, those challenges are balanced by incredible gifts—gifts that shape your personality, values, and approach to life. Sensitivity allows you to notice details others miss, to tune in to emotions and environments, and to feel compassion in ways that make you a source of comfort and understanding for others. Embracing these qualities means fully stepping into who you are, honoring your natural strengths, and using them to create a life that's meaningful and fulfilling.

Remember that the world needs highly sensitive people. Your ability to empathize, to listen deeply, and to offer comfort are qualities that can transform relationships and communities. In work, sensitivity allows you to bring creativity, intuition, and insight into your projects, helping you think innovatively and connect ideas others may overlook. In friendships and family, your sensitivity helps others feel seen, understood, and valued. Embracing your sensitivity means understanding that these strengths aren't "nice-to-haves"—they're qualities that are deeply impactful, even if they're not always acknowledged in traditional ways.

Reframing Sensitivity as Your Superpower
Think of your sensitivity as a superpower. Like any powerful trait, it comes with both responsibilities and gifts. When used intentionally, it can guide you to form genuine connections, experience a profound sense of purpose, and achieve a state of harmony in your life that's both nourishing and empowering. Embracing sensitivity means releasing any shame or doubt you may have held and recognizing it as a unique and valuable part of your identity.

To reframe your sensitivity as a superpower, practice these steps:

1. **Recognize Your Unique Strengths**: Identify the qualities that sensitivity brings to your life—whether that's empathy, creativity, a love of beauty, or a desire for justice. Reflect on how these strengths have positively influenced your life and others' lives.

2. **Acknowledge the Value of Your Perspective**: Recognize that being sensitive offers you a unique perspective that can add meaning and depth to any situation. Remind yourself of times when your insights, empathy, or attention to detail made a difference. Value these moments as evidence of the power of sensitivity.

3. **Embrace Your Needs as Essential to Your Well-Being**: Sensitivity comes with specific needs, from downtime to

decompression. Embracing sensitivity means honoring these needs unapologetically, recognizing that they allow you to recharge and offer your best self to the world.

4. **Set Intentions for Using Your Gifts**: Choose to consciously use your sensitivity to make a difference, whether that's through nurturing relationships, bringing compassion to your work, or engaging in creative pursuits that bring you joy. Setting intentions gives you a sense of purpose and helps you channel your sensitivity in ways that feel meaningful.

Creating Your HSP Superpower Blueprint

As you move forward, consider creating a personal blueprint to help you live in a way that honors and celebrates your sensitivity. This "HSP Superpower Blueprint" is your guide to implementing what you've learned in this book and using your sensitivity as a guiding force. Here's a step-by-step approach to creating a life plan that lets you thrive as a Highly Sensitive Person:

1. **Define Your Core Values and Goals**
Begin by identifying your core values. These are the principles that guide you, inspire you, and resonate with you on a deep level. For HSPs, values often include compassion, integrity, creativity, and authenticity. Next, set meaningful goals that align with these values. Consider each area of your life—relationships, career, personal growth, and well-being—and set intentions that will help you live in harmony with your sensitivity. Ask yourself questions like:
- How can I nurture my relationships in a way that feels fulfilling and aligned with my sensitivity?
- What kind of work environment and tasks allow me to feel valued and engaged?
- What self-care practices help me recharge and maintain balance?

2. **Create a Supportive Environment**
Design your physical and emotional environments to support your sensitivity. This could include creating quiet, comfortable spaces for reflection, using tools like white noise machines to

manage sensory input, or setting boundaries in relationships to protect your energy. Be intentional about surrounding yourself with people who appreciate and respect your sensitivity. A supportive environment nurtures your well-being and gives you the energy to embrace and use your superpower.

3. Develop a Self-Care Toolkit

Self-care is essential for HSPs, and having a reliable toolkit can make a big difference in managing stress and maintaining balance. Include practices that soothe, restore, and energize you, such as meditation, journaling, time in nature, or creative activities. Self-care also includes honoring your boundaries, practicing gratitude, and reminding yourself regularly of the gifts of sensitivity.

4. Set Boundaries and Practice Assertiveness

Boundaries are essential for protecting your energy and ensuring that your sensitivity remains a source of strength. Practice saying "no" when needed, ask for space to recharge, and communicate your needs to others with kindness and clarity. Assertiveness doesn't come naturally to all HSPs, but it can be learned and will empower you to honor your boundaries while still showing respect for others.

5. Create Long-Term Growth Goals

Growth is an essential part of well-being, and it's especially important for HSPs who thrive on self-reflection and personal development. Set long-term goals that will challenge you and allow you to explore new depths within yourself. This could include deepening your relationships, learning new skills that align with your values, or pursuing a passion project. Growth goals help you continue evolving while honoring your true self.

6. Reflect and Adjust Regularly

Life is ever-changing, and your needs as an HSP may evolve over time. Schedule regular check-ins with yourself to review your goals, evaluate your self-care practices, and make adjustments as needed. Use journaling, meditation, or other reflective practices to stay in touch with your inner self, ensuring that your blueprint remains aligned with who you are becoming.

Final Encouragement for HSPs: Celebrating Your Superpower

As you close this book and step forward, know that your journey as a Highly Sensitive Person is just beginning. The awareness you've cultivated, the tools you've gained, and the intentions you've set will guide you as you continue to embrace your sensitivity. You have a superpower—a unique gift that brings richness to life, that nurtures compassion in others, and that creates beauty, peace, and meaning in a world that needs all these things.

You are capable of thriving, of finding fulfillment, and of living in harmony with your true self. Embrace the power of your sensitivity as a gift not just for you but for those you touch along the way. Sensitivity isn't a weakness to overcome; it's a strength to cherish, a source of wisdom, and a reminder of what it means to live deeply.

Take pride in your journey, and remember that by embracing your sensitivity, you're contributing something valuable and unique to the world. You are not alone; there is a community of HSPs who share your experiences and are here to support you. Together, we can create a world that honors the beauty of sensitivity, celebrating it as the superpower it truly is.

Bonus Resources

Congratulations on completing this guidebook and beginning your journey toward embracing your sensitivity as a superpower. This process of growth and self-awareness is ongoing, and to help you continue thriving, we've compiled additional resources—practical worksheets and exercises, recommended reading, and support networks—that will guide you as you further explore and nurture your HSP traits. These resources are here to support you as you integrate everything you've learned and create a life that honors your sensitivity while empowering you to thrive.

Practical Worksheets and Exercises

These tools are designed to help you manage overwhelm, set healthy boundaries, and cultivate self-compassion—core practices that support the highly sensitive experience. Use these worksheets regularly to reinforce your learning and continue building a life that honors your unique needs.

1. **Overwhelm Management Worksheet:**
Overwhelm is a common experience for HSPs, especially in environments filled with sensory input or emotional intensity. This worksheet helps you identify when you're feeling overwhelmed, pinpoint specific triggers, and develop personalized strategies to regain balance. It encourages mindfulness and gives you tools for recognizing when to step back and recharge.

2. **Boundary Setting Worksheet:**
Healthy boundaries are essential for protecting your energy and living in alignment with your needs. This worksheet helps you reflect on areas of your life—whether in relationships, work, or self-care—where boundaries need to be established or reinforced. It also provides practical strategies for setting those boundaries assertively, with kindness and clarity. Sample scripts are included to assist you in communicating your needs in a way that is compassionate and respectful.

3. Self-Compassion Journal Prompts:
Practicing self-compassion is vital for HSPs, especially since sensitivity can sometimes lead to self-criticism or doubt. These journal prompts are designed to help you reflect on moments of self-compassion and explore how to develop a more supportive relationship with yourself. By regularly engaging with these prompts, you can build a foundation of kindness and understanding that nurtures your emotional well-being.

4. Energy-Tracking Exercise:
This exercise helps you track your energy throughout the day, identifying activities or interactions that leave you feeling drained versus those that replenish you. By recognizing your energy patterns, you'll gain a clearer understanding of what drains you and what energizes you, allowing you to prioritize the activities that promote balance and well-being.

Additional Online Resources

Below is a collection of podcasts and online resources that dive deeper into the HSP experience, offering valuable insights and practical advice. These resources can help you continue to nurture your personal growth and connect with the broader community of highly sensitive individuals.

1. Podcasts:
- **HSP Revolution** by Kelly O'Laughlin: A podcast dedicated to helping HSPs thrive, offering practical advice and interviews with experts on topics like self-care, boundaries, and emotional resilience.
- **The Sensitive Empowerment Podcast** by Julie Bjelland: This podcast is focused on empowering HSPs through discussions on self-care, intuition, creativity, and emotional growth.
- **The Highly Sensitive Person Podcast**: This podcast offers tips and support for navigating the world as a sensitive person, focusing on the challenges and strengths of the HSP experience.

2. Online Resources:

- **Highly Sensitive Refuge** (highlysensitiverefuge.com): A website dedicated to providing articles, tools, and resources for HSPs. It's a place to learn, share experiences, and find community support.
- **The Empathic World** (theempathicworld.com): This platform offers resources and guidance for empaths and HSPs, with practical advice on emotional protection, energy management, and self-care.
- **HSP Global Community** (hspglobalcommunity.com): An online community and resource hub that offers educational materials and personal growth tools specifically for HSPs.

Support Networks for HSPs

Connecting with others who share your experiences is one of the most powerful ways to feel supported, understood, and validated. Below are several organizations, online communities, and forums where you can find solidarity, share experiences, and access support as you continue to thrive as an HSP.

1. Online Communities:
- **The Highly Sensitive Person Facebook Group**: A vibrant online community where HSPs come together to share experiences, ask questions, and offer mutual support. This group provides a sense of connection and camaraderie, making it a great place to seek advice and encouragement.
- **HSP Support Network on Reddit**: A community on Reddit for HSPs to discuss their experiences, share coping strategies, and learn from each other. It's a welcoming space for HSPs to engage in conversations about all aspects of their lives.

2. Support Groups and Meetups:
- **HSP Meetup Groups**: Many cities offer in-person or virtual Meetup groups where HSPs can gather and share their experiences. You can search for local meetups through **Meetup.com**, or find online groups that offer virtual meetings.
- **Therapists Specializing in HSPs**: Many therapists specialize in working with HSPs and can help you navigate challenges with personalized support. Searching online directories like

Psychology Today can help you find professionals who understand the unique needs of sensitive individuals.

3. **Organizations:**
- **The Highly Sensitive Person Network**: A global organization focused on providing resources, events, and a sense of community for HSPs. The network offers support and guidance, helping you to better understand and embrace your sensitivity.
- **The Empathic Society**: An organization that focuses on helping empaths and HSPs thrive by providing workshops, educational events, and community-building opportunities.

Final Thoughts

As you continue on your journey as an HSP, remember that you are not alone. The world is filled with people who share your experiences and understand the unique gifts and challenges of sensitivity. The resources in this section are designed to provide you with ongoing support, tools, and inspiration as you continue to thrive in your own way.

By embracing your sensitivity, honoring your needs, and connecting with others who share your path, you can create a life that is both fulfilling and empowering. Continue to practice self-compassion, set boundaries that protect your energy, and engage with communities that nurture your well-being. Your sensitivity is a superpower—use it to build the life you deserve.

Take the time to explore the resources shared here, and remember that this journey is ongoing. You are always evolving, growing, and finding new ways to embrace your sensitivity with grace and strength. Your unique perspective and gifts are needed in this world, and by caring for yourself and connecting with others, you will continue to thrive and make a positive impact.

Thank you for joining me in this exploration of what it means to be a Highly Sensitive Person. You have everything you need within you to live a life that honors your sensitivity and empowers you to be the best version of yourself. Here's to your continued growth, peace, and fulfillment.